In *Thirsty for a Miracle*, Greg Allgood demonstrates that it's possible to live a life full of grand adventure and purpose. By sharing his journey with us, Greg shows how he has overcome challenges with a relentless focus in pursuing his God-sized goal of ending the global water crisis. This is a story of putting faith into action to provide hope, life, and a future for millions of people.

BOB GOFF, *New York Times* bestselling author, coach, and chaser of whimsy

I have long been a deep believer in the importance of *human agency*, the difference that an individual can make. Rarely have I seen a story that brings this more vividly to life than that which Greg Allgood tells in his book, *Thirsty for a Miracle*. His passionate commitment to providing clear and safe water to people in desperate need of it emerges from this story, step-by-step in his life and career. He has followed his vision, his commitment, and his calling every step of the way. And countless millions of people have benefited from it. This is a story of adventure, a challenge overcome, and challenges still to meet. It is written in a highly engaging, personal way. I guarantee that you will be moved by Greg's story. I heartily recommend that you read it.

JOHN E. PEPPER, JR., former CEO, Procter & Gamble; former chairman, The Walt Disney Company

As a former civil engineer turned missions pastor, I was reminded by Greg's story that each of us can make a meaningful difference in addressing a very solvable global problem. I've long understood the life-changing impact clean water has on a community, and Greg captures that big-picture reality through a compelling personal narrative. Having seen World Vision's work in Rwanda firsthand, I can't think of a more powerful or practical way to live out the gospel than by transforming lives and strengthening communities through access to clean water.

TOM WHEELER, missions director, Saddleback Church

I've known Greg Allgood as someone who doesn't just talk about making a difference—he actually does it. His work bringing clean water and hope to communities around the world is a powerful example of what servant leadership looks like in action. Greg leads with integrity, intelligence, and a genuine care for people, and his life shows us that one person truly can be a powerful force for good and change the world for the better. I'm proud to endorse his story.

BOB McDONALD, former chairman, president, and CEO, Procter & Gamble; eighth US Secretary of Veterans Affairs

Greg's work has changed countless lives by expanding access to clean water. Through Sesame Workshop's partnership with World Vision on water, sanitation, and hygiene initiatives, I've had the opportunity to witness his thoughtful leadership in action. He has been a tireless champion for ensuring that women and girls, who are often the most affected by lack of water, have access to this vital resource.

SHERRIE WESTIN, president and CEO, Sesame Workshop

I've known Greg Allgood for many years and have always admired the way he combines science, purpose, and heart to be a force for good. What began as an idea inside P&G—to turn innovation into a tool for good—became, through Greg's leadership and passion, a movement that brought clean water to millions around the world. Everyone striving for a better world should read *Thirsty for a Miracle*—not just to be inspired by Greg's impact, but to discover the life lessons it holds for all of us about the impact of using our own passion to make the world better.

MARC PRITCHARD, Chief Brand Officer, Procter & Gamble

What an incredibly powerful book! I loved reading the story of how God used Greg Allgood to literally change the lives of millions. I promise this book will fill your cup.

DEBBIE MACOMBER, #1 *New York Times* bestselling author

Greg's story is the story of those he's served. He grew from doubting that God could to trusting that he would on his journey into becoming God's water boy. As Dr. Allgood quenched the thirst of millions, his own thirst was quenched by seeing miracles unfold through his surrender to the goodness of God. The "aw-shucks" conversational style of this big-hearted man from the heart of North Carolina belies a keen mind and a steely determination to bring life-giving water to those accustomed to drinking alongside cattle. I read the book in two days, and more than once his authentic humanity caused water to flow from my eyes as purely as it pours from the World Vision waterpoints.

BARRY ROWAN, business leader and author of *The Spiritual Art of Business: Connecting the Daily with the Divine*

As a follower of Jesus, I have always believed that God works through ordinary people to change the world. Just look at Joseph, Moses, David, Esther, and Peter. If you think that He can't use you, you need to read Greg Allgood's story. Greg led the effort to bring clean water to more than thirty-five million of the world's poorest people—and still counting! God can use you, too. When we make ourselves completely available and dare to dream big dreams, God makes the impossible possible.

RICHARD STEARNS, president emeritus of World Vision, author of *The Hole in Our Gospel*

It is impossible to read *Thirsty for a Miracle* and not be moved. Greg Allgood's transformation—from a research scientist at Procter & Gamble to a singular force in helping tens of millions of people have access to clean water—is a story of faith, persistence, collaboration, creativity, and hope. Greg's life story proves that one person can indeed make an enormous difference. His book will undoubtedly inspire others to find their purpose and make their difference in this world.

JIM STENGEL, former global marketing officer, Procter & Gamble; host of *The CMO Podcast*; and author of *Grow*

Thirsty for a Miracle by Greg Allgood is a must-read for anyone seeking inspiration to make a meaningful impact in the world. Greg's journey is a heartfelt story of resilience, faith, and dedication and a powerful reminder of how one person aligning their talents and passion can make a difference in the lives of millions. He has literally earned the title "Water Boy." This book is a great testament of his life's work but also an invitation for us to join the mission of solving the global water crisis.

HARMON KONG, author of *Values Over Valuables*

Greg Allgood has written a book that is enjoyable and educational, inspirational and practical. Give this book to anyone who wonders if their career can have greater meaning and every young person looking for work that matters. Greg's personal story shows how God can use us all to change the world.

DALE HANSON BOURKE, author of *Strong Girls, Strong World,* former board member, World Vision US & International

In *Thirsty for a Miracle*, Greg Allgood invites us into a story of generosity that is not abstract or theoretical but lived out through obedience, perseverance, and risk-taking for a greater cause. He shares his journey through professional and personal disappointments and achievements, ultimately leading to a life of purpose shaped by faith, humility, and service to the world's most vulnerable people. Greg's story is a powerful reminder that each one of us can meaningfully impact our world when we apply our expertise, follow our passions, and faithfully pursue the adventures God invites us into.

APRIL CHAPMAN, CEO of Generous Giving

Heartbreaking and inspirational from the very first page. But more than that, *Thirsty for a Miracle* shows how much good we can do in the world when we have a purpose, a plan, and a belief in something bigger than ourselves.

CINDY DiBIASI, cofounder of 3D Communications

Thirsty for a Miracle is not Greg Allgood's story. It is God's. It is not World Vision's story. It is God's story of using fallible people and organizations to accomplish His purposes. This could be a technical account of clean water needs and methods. Rather, it is a story of humor, failure, setbacks, miracles, weakness, and especially of remarkable and powerful women and men in desperate circumstances struggling to live with dirty water and then seeing the miracle of wells and water packets transform their lives. In the midst of this journey, seeing Greg's faith and humanity being transformed as God uses him to be a key part of bringing clean water and as a witness for Jesus to millions around the world is also a miracle.

JERRY WHITE, PhD, international president emeritus, The Navigators

Thirsty for a Miracle

THIRSTY FOR A MIRACLE

They Needed Clean Water.
He Needed True Purpose.
An Inspiring Story of Hope
and Transformation.

GREG ALLGOOD

TYNDALE
REFRESH™
Think Well. Live Well. Be Well.

Visit Tyndale online at tyndale.com.

Thirsty for a Miracle: They Needed Clean Water. He Needed True Purpose. An Inspiring Story of Hope and Transformation.

Cover design by Faceout Studio, Addie Lutzo

Interior design by Cathy Miller

Edited by Jonathan Schindler

Library of Congress Cataloging-in-Publication Data

A catalog record for this book is available from the Library of Congress.

ISBN 979-8-4005-1371-8

Printed in the United States of America

32 31 30 29 28 27 26
7 6 5 4 3 2 1

This book is dedicated to Wes Williams and Don Glenn, two of the best friends anyone could wish to have. As we say about our friendship, "We've gone too far to turn around now."

I was thirsty, and you gave me a drink.

MATTHEW 25:35

Contents

Foreword

I'll never forget the celebration in May 2023 in Kageyo, Rwanda. Throngs of people filled two massive tents, and more spilled out onto the surrounding hillsides. There were speeches and testimonials, prayers and praises, live music and dancing. I found myself in a sea of kids wearing World Vision–orange shirts. Together we raised our fists and joyfully chanted, "ONE MILLION!"

We were celebrating the milestone of World Vision reaching more than one million people across Rwanda with access to clean water. It was the exciting completion of a big, audacious goal set five years before—known as "Finish the Job"—and proof of concept that World Vision could provide access to clean water to everyone, everywhere we work in a country.

Somewhere in the crowd was one of the key catalysts of Finish the Job: Greg Allgood.

Greg and I have had similar career trajectories. Our professional tactics were forged in the crucible of Procter & Gamble's culture of excellence. We both embraced breakthrough innovation to drive not only profits but also social good. As corporate executives, we were driven by self-reliance—until the Holy Spirit intervened, leading us to a deeper walk with Jesus and eventually a call to Christian ministry.

I arrived at World Vision a few years after Greg, where he had already established a thriving partnership with our former employer around the P&G Purifier of Water packets. The packets were ideal as an immediate water solution in some of the difficult places World Vision works—conflict zones, areas hit by natural disasters, and communities where other interventions have failed. P&G's packets became vital to World Vision's "bridge strategy," providing clean water in the short term while we worked alongside communities to empower them with a permanent, sustainable water system.

Greg had also hit the ground running to contribute to World Vision's first comprehensive five-year business plan for our water work. He then helped us achieve the dream of World Vision becoming the largest nongovernmental provider of clean drinking water, with an incredible impact of reaching one new person with access to clean water *every 10 seconds*.

This was remarkable work. But as I got to know Greg better, I came to understand that clean water is more than a career focus for him. It is his passion, his calling, and his life mission.

That's why he's willing to fly millions of miles and log countless hours on treacherous roads to reach the world's hardest-to-reach places. Why, even after appearing on TV with Oprah Winfrey, he's equally proud to share the spotlight with a mom in rural Ghana. The people Greg has encountered on more than sixty visits to Africa have made a deep impression on him, fueling his passion to empower them with access to life-giving clean water.

God is using all of Greg in this mission: his background in science, his flair for marketing and promotion, his ability to connect with donors, and his relentless pursuit for impact. I've watched him serve not for recognition but for results for children, mothers, and communities, who now have hope and health because of his work. His journey—from a scientist with big ambitions to a servant leader known as "God's water boy"—is a testimony to what the Lord can accomplish through a willing heart.

The title of this book is appropriate. I believe that when we become instruments of God's redemptive work in the world, we can *expect* miracles. For example, some years ago I visited a community in Ethiopia where clean water was once scarce, yet multiple drilling attempts by various organizations had all failed. When World Vision came to try, the people had reason to doubt. But they were *thirsty for a miracle.* "The Lord will bring us water," they said, and they dedicated themselves to prayer and fasting as the drilling commenced—days and days, deeper and deeper. At an astonishing depth of 318 meters, water gushed up! Appropriately, the people named it the Well of Prayer.

Greg has experienced this "pressing into the miraculous," as I call it, witnessing transcendent moments such as clean water bursting from the parched earth, prompting decisions for Christ, and the miraculous provision of funds from people moved by the Holy Spirit. You'll find compelling stories like these woven throughout Greg's book. Once you start reading, you won't want to stop!

Thirsty for a Miracle illustrates that clean water is more than a physical need. It is a tangible expression of God's love flowing through us, pointing to the ultimate source of life: Jesus Christ.

Edgar Sandoval Sr.
President and CEO of World Vision, Inc.

Author's Note

This book is a memoir. It reflects my present recollections of experiences over time. Some names and characteristics have been changed, some events have been compressed, and some dialogue has been recreated. That being said, everything in this book is true to the best of my knowledge, and most of the events can be verified in blogs, news releases, videos, and newspaper stories.

The profits from this book will be donated to World Vision Water.

Prologue

The last thing I expected was to watch a miracle unfold before my eyes.

I was more than a decade into my career at Procter & Gamble, and I was feeling restless. It felt like I'd had few discernible wins. I was wondering what was next.

I had joined P&G in 1986 as a scientist working on product safety and had recently been transferred to P&G's personal care division, lured by the prospect of working on a new water purification packet and helping to alleviate the world's water crisis.

In the summer of 2003, I flew to Kenya. P&G was conducting a clinical trial on the purification packet in cooperation with the US Centers for Disease Control and Prevention, and I was there to see how people used it in real-world conditions.

Once in the country, I rode in a truck to reach a rural village where people lived in extreme poverty. Most lived in huts made of sticks and mud with straw roofs. They were subsistence farmers scratching out their living from the red clay fields by growing corn and beans.

When I got to the village, I learned that the people who lived there had no clean water source in the area. They had identified a low area about a mile away and dug out a pond using their farming tools.

It filled up in the rainy season, and they hoped and prayed the water would last through the dry season. They walked a mile to the pond for water and then walked a mile back carrying heavy containers. If the pond dried out before the rains came back, they had to walk an additional mile each way to a different pond.

It was mostly women and girls who took these essential, time-consuming walks every day. They completed this round trip early in the morning and then again in the evening. Every day of the year. No time off for weekends or holidays.

I accompanied the water walkers to the pond and watched from the banks as a woman scooped up water. Her name, I learned, was Mercy. She was thirty-four years old, although she looked older. She was wearing tattered clothes and was gathering the water with her teenage son and five-year-old daughter. Each of them had a yellow bucket—a reused cooking oil container. Mercy's bucket had a narrow opening at the top and held twenty liters, so it weighed forty-four pounds when full. Her son also had a twenty-liter bucket, though his had an open top because the lid had broken and was thrown away. He had to perform quite a balancing act to carry this bucket without spilling. Her young daughter had a ten-liter bucket, so she struggled to carry a load of twenty-two pounds—probably half her own weight or more—the mile back to their home.

Mercy left her sandals on the bank as she waded through the mud to a deeper part of the pond to collect water. The water was the color of clay. Mercy used her son's open bucket to skim water off the surface and avoid putting mud directly into her bucket. It took her several minutes to fill up her bucket, and then she filled up her daughter's. She used a small cup to top off her son's bucket.

As Mercy and her children were gathering their water, a small herd of cows joined them in the pond. Several of the animals relieved themselves as they entered the water. Mercy had no choice but to gather water from the cows' bathroom. Cow dung lay all along the banks of the pond. Its pungent smell filled the air. It was clear this was a normal occurrence.

This dirty pond was the only water source for Mercy and her family—for cooking, bathing, and even drinking. Mercy had to either let her kids die of dehydration or risk illness (and potentially death) from the bacteria, viruses, and parasites in the water. It was a devastating choice for a mother to have to make.

And she was far from alone in facing such a dilemma.

By this time, I had learned some facts about the global water crisis. In the early 2000s, more than two billion people around the world lacked access to a clean water source. An estimated four thousand children under the age of five were dying *every day* from contaminated water—more child deaths than those caused by HIV/AIDS and malaria combined.

And the world was not outraged at this enormous death toll. Partly this was because people in the developed world had clean water themselves and simply didn't *see* the problem. Partly it was because most people didn't realize solutions to this crisis were available if the world had the will to implement them. So although many of us had heard something about the illness and death caused by unsafe water, we let ourselves become numb to the numbers.

It was impossible to remain numb when I faced *one* family—*one* mom, *one* son, *one* daughter—who had no choice but to drink unsafe water.

I approached Mercy. Through an interpreter, I asked, "Would it be all right if I showed you a new way for cleaning water?"

She nodded.

I emptied the powder from one of the tea-bag-sized P&G packets into the boy's open-lidded bucket of dirty water and stirred. The powder worked like a dirt magnet, removing dirt particles, worms, and parasites. After thirty minutes, the water was crystal clear, completely purified, and the bacteria and viruses were killed. I poured the water through a cloth, and when it was ready, I drank it.

Mercy's eyes grew wide when she saw how clean the pond water had become. I offered it to her, and she drank, as did her daughter and son. They may never have had such clean water in their lives.

I am a scientist, and though I was thoroughly familiar with how the packets worked, I was amazed myself. I had already seen the packets used in Guatemala, Pakistan, and Morocco, but in those places the water already looked clear, even though it wasn't safe. Here the contamination was visible. This was the first time I observed in a real-life situation very muddy water turned clear. And the experience of *seeing* dirty water become clean felt like magic. No, it felt like a *miracle*.

But what really got to me was Mercy's reaction.

To my embarrassment, she got down on her hands and knees. "Can I have some of these packets?" Mercy begged.

I could see on Mercy's face, and hear in her voice, the understanding that this was a matter of life and death for her and her family. She knew full well that the pond water had been making them sick. She told me later that her children frequently missed school because they had persistent, painful diarrhea. When the pond went dry, her children missed school again simply because they were too tired from hauling water from the more distant pond.

Although I had *known* the facts about the global water crisis, now I *felt* them. With Mercy there before me, the full weight of the crisis hit me. It was a matter of life and death for millions of people *just like her*.

That encounter with Mercy altered my life irrevocably. I had been trying to discover what my purpose was. Now I understood that helping to solve the world's water crisis was not just a piece of my corporate job; it was my life's calling. I had the most amazing opportunity to make a difference in the world by addressing this great need.

I didn't know at the time what shape this calling would take. I couldn't see all the ways God had prepared me for where he'd put me. I had no idea the places God would take me or the obstacles I would face. I had no clue that, in giving me this calling, God would also reveal my blind spots and character flaws, refining me in the process. All I knew was that, from here on out, I was resolute in my commitment to do everything I could for the Mercys of the world.

There was no going back.

1

IT'S ALL GOOD

I was born in 1959 in the central North Carolina community of Cary. Back then, Cary was a small town quickly expanding with people joining businesses in the Research Triangle Park or with people working at North Carolina State, Duke, or UNC–Chapel Hill. My mom, Peggy, was a schoolteacher, and my dad, Jim, worked at NC State as part of the network of North Carolina farm extension agents tasked with helping farmers improve their businesses.

My brother, Jimmy, and I had the freedom to ride our bikes all over town and play sports with the neighborhood kids. We went to Cary First Baptist Church on Sundays, visited our relatives in the foothills of North Carolina, and made the occasional trip to the beach or mountains.

I started the Boy Scouts program at an early age and became an Eagle Scout at thirteen, at least a couple of years ahead of the typical schedule. Through scouting I developed a love of the outdoors. As much as I loved it, though, scouting also nearly ended my life.

On a camping trip, I broke a fundamental rule: I fell asleep with a lit candle in my tent. In the middle of the night, I was awakened from what felt like a deep sleep by my friend and tentmate, Thad Banks.

"The tent's on fire! Greg, the tent's on fire!"

As I woke, I found that I was no longer in the blazing tent but huddled next to a tree outside it. Confused, I jumped up, ran over to the tent, and stomped out the fire with my bare feet.

When the flames had died down and the night was dark again, I realized I was in a great deal of pain. Thad switched on his flashlight. My skin was charred on my right arm and leg.

We ran and woke up our scout leaders, who drove me to the hospital. My hand and thigh had third-degree burns. I was treated and put in bandages. While this was a frightening experience, in a way I was proud that I had survived, and I looked at my scars as a merit badge to show off.

Once I was recovering back home, my scoutmaster, Frank Goodrum, came to visit me, carrying a paper sack. He was a big, calloused man who for some reason always called me Craig.

After he'd checked up on me a bit, he said, "Let me show you something, Craig." He handed me the sack. I looked inside and saw an unidentifiable wad of charred and smoky-smelling fabric. I looked at Frank, puzzled. Frank reached over and fished out a blackened zipper. "This is all that's left of your sleeping bag."

It was sobering to think I had been inside that sleeping bag while it was burning.

Frank continued, "You must have fallen asleep, and your bag caught on fire from the candle you were burning."

"Why didn't I wake up?" I asked.

"You and Thad must have inhaled too much smoke."

"Even though my skin was getting charred?" I had a hard time believing that.

"You probably became unconscious."

"Then how did we get out at all?"

"My best guess," Frank said, "is that the fire grew big enough to burn through the rope that held up your tent. Once the tent fell in, the fresh air must have woken you up."

I didn't remember any of this. I must have been in shock from the burns and crawled over to the tree when I woke up.

"You can expect disciplinary action for breaking the rule about using a candle in the tent," Frank said. Then he looked me in the eye. He was determined that I heard what he had to say. "Craig, you should be dead. Either the smoke inhalation or the burning sleeping bag should have killed you."

With tremendous conviction he added, "Only a miracle could have saved your life. God saved you for a reason, Craig. God must have a plan for your life to make a difference, and that's why the fire didn't kill you."

Frank's prophetic words didn't mean much to me at the time, not least because he couldn't get my name right. But I carried them with me. It would take me many years—encompassing half my career—to resurrect this thought and really understand God's plan for me to make a difference in this world. "Craig" didn't get it, but eventually Greg would.

My best friend growing up was Wes Williams. I don't remember ever meeting Wes. Our mothers attended UNC Greensboro at the same time and became friends. They both married men who were employed at NC State and moved to Cary when its population was only a few hundred people. They started families and attended Cary

First Baptist Church together. They played women's and couples' bridge together every month. Because they became lifelong friends, so did their families.

Wes and I were constantly together. The Williamses lived in the cul-de-sac right behind our home, and by cutting through my backyard and a neighbor's, I could be at Wes's house in a couple of minutes. Wes and I would watch television shows after school with his sisters. I was at their house so often that Wes's dad would tease, "Are you living with us now?"

Both our families had season tickets for NC State games, and Wes and I would frequently sit together. Wes had such a loud clap that his dad told him he couldn't clap unless he toned it down. Since both our dads worked at NC State, we had access to the Faculty Club swimming pool and spent many summer days playing together there. We were both avid basketball players. We played every chance we had, playing half-court at my house or at First Baptist's indoor court or Cary Presbyterian's outdoor one.

It was while playing basketball at Cary Presbyterian with Wes that I first met Don Glenn. Don's family had moved in close to Cary Presbyterian, so he would play basketball there. Don, like Wes, was a year ahead of me in school, so he and Wes soon shared several of the same classes and hung out together at school. As a result, Don was more Wes's friend than mine, but because Wes was so welcoming, soon the three of us were inseparable.

One night when we were in high school, Don and Wes were hanging out at Wes's house. Don had driven his 1969 Chevrolet Camaro and left it unlocked. Another friend and I were waiting outside.

A common prank at the time was to let out the clutch of a friend's car and then roll it to another location. This opportunity was too good to ignore. My friend suggested, "Hey, why don't we roll Don's car?"

It seemed like such a harmless prank that I agreed. We started moving Don's Camaro, but as we were rolling it, we lost control. Don's car hit a telephone pole. The sound brought Wes and Don running out of the house. When Don saw what had happened, he was furious. The passenger door of Don's Camaro was visibly damaged.

And, it turned out, the damage was even worse than it looked. The cost of repairs was beyond what the car was worth. The cost was also more than the money I'd saved from my job parking cars and cleaning up after football games. I knew my relationship with Don was in jeopardy.

I asked my dad for help, and he negotiated with Don's dad for a solution. My dad offered a fair price to Don's dad to buy the car from him. Don's dad accepted.

My dad put an ad in the paper to sell the car at a price that would mean my other friend and I would have to work summer jobs to pay for the difference between the sale price and what my father paid Don's dad. I was home when first one and then a second guy showed up to make an offer on the Camaro. They got into a bidding war, and it looked like we were going to make a profit on the prank. My dad knew that was not the lesson he wanted us to learn, so he sold the car for the asking price to the first guy who showed up, and my friend and I worked off the difference.

Don and his dad had enough to buy Don a new car, but it wasn't a Camaro. Don was heartbroken at the loss of his awesome wheels, but he eventually forgave me for ruining his car.

While I regret totaling Don's car, this experience was the turning point in our friendship. It was no longer that Don was just Wes's friend. Don and I became close friends ourselves.

Prior to college, I made good grades in school without much effort. Near the end of my junior year, I knew that if I was one of the top ten juniors academically, I would not have to take final exams and could be a junior marshal to help with the seniors' graduation.

That meant I'd be able to hang out with my two best friends during their important time. That was strong enough motivation for me to make the grades.

But making the grades also made me smug. When I was goofing around in Ms. Thomas's advanced math class, she called me out. "This information is going to be on the final exam!" she warned.

I replied sassily, "I don't really care. I'm a junior marshal and don't have to take the exam."

"Go wait in the hallway," Ms. Thomas instructed me. She wanted privacy for what she had to say to me. "Your cockiness is going to catch up with you, Greg," she told me. "Someday you'll learn that you need more than your own smarts to succeed in life." Up to that point, I *had* been able to succeed on my own, so I didn't take what she said to heart. But as with my scout leader's "prophecy," years later I would understand just what her words meant.

By the time my friends graduated, I had a general plan for my career. I wanted to be involved in science—a natural enough goal for someone who grew up near Research Triangle Park. But more than that, I wanted a life of adventure, travel, and making an impact.

Through television, two global citizens became my role models. I loved how Jacques Cousteau invented scuba and traveled the world teaching millions the importance of preserving our oceans. I was also fascinated by Jane Goodall, who spent years at Gombe Stream National Park in Tanzania, going much deeper into understanding chimpanzee behavior than humans had ever gone before. It wasn't only their adventures that captivated me but also their ability to tell stories that made science come to life. Science, I came to understand, wasn't a dull subject to be endured in school. It had real-life implications, if only people could be made to see it.

Jacques Cousteau and Jane Goodall inspired me to see how one person could make a difference in the world through science. So in 1977 I followed Don to the University of North Carolina–Chapel

Hill, where I earned a bachelor's degree and a master's degree in public health, focusing on water research. Then, because funding became available, I moved on to NC State, where I earned a degree in toxicology. My interest in the program was driven by the fact that it was multidisciplinary, requiring significant knowledge in biochemistry, epidemiology, and microbiology, among other areas. I realized that much of the breakthrough thinking I admired usually happened not deeply immersed in one area of knowledge but at the intersection of several. I didn't want to be pigeonholed into a limited number of experiences but craved the kind of holistic knowledge that led to real-life solutions.

My PhD dissertation dealt with the effects of oxygen on the thermophilic bacteria found at Old Faithful geyser. Again, inspired by Cousteau and Goodall, I made it my mission to explain my research to nonscientists so they could understand the practical benefits of the work.

Throughout college, graduate studies, and beyond, Wes, Don, and I have remained close, lifelong friends.

Now that I was finishing my academic career, I knew I needed to find a job. I heard about Procter & Gamble from a college friend who had joined P&G the prior year. I loved the idea of working for one of the great American companies and decided to investigate. I got hold of the book *Eyes on Tomorrow: The Evolution of Procter & Gamble*. I read about how P&G's growth over 150 years at that point closely matched the history of much of the United States since radio and then television became successes partly because of P&G–sponsored soap operas. When I applied for a job there, my knowledge of the company impressed my interviewers. They wondered why this recent science graduate was asking them about P&G marketing strategy and management structures.

I was offered a position in the beauty care division. When I received the offer, I was ecstatic. I could see myself having a long and successful career there. But my job offer was in Cincinnati, Ohio. I am a seventh-generation North Carolinian. My whole family, as well as Wes, still lived in North Carolina. (Don had moved to Florida for a job.) As much as I hated to leave, the offer was enough for me to move away from my beloved North Carolina home.

At first I occupied lower-level positions in the beauty care and health divisions of the company, helping to ensure the safety of products like shampoos and soaps. It was a long way from the undersea world of Jacques Cousteau and the banks of Gombe Stream National Park with Jane Goodall, but I loved that my efforts helped ensure that products used by billions of people were safe.

I thoroughly enjoyed my work in the beauty care division, but I also yearned for more adventure and set my sights on international travel. I looked for opportunities to volunteer for anything associated with P&G's international business. At first, this involved helping our international new hires learn about P&G and hosting them at P&G's headquarters in Cincinnati. This allowed me to learn about different cultures and how to work effectively with a diverse group of people, and I loved it. After a while, my work supporting our international staff led to trips overseas.

In 1990 I switched over to the food and beverage division, where I joined a team of scientists seeking approval in the United States and globally for the controversial fat replacer olestra. I didn't know it at the time, but my work with olestra would prove instrumental to finding my calling in working to solve the world's water crisis.

2

THE OPRAH WINFREY SHOW

I had never been more keyed up and eager to get something started than when I walked onto the stage of *The Oprah Winfrey Show* as Oprah's guest. Oprah herself was there in a gray suit and with fashionably styled hair, already an icon and a world-renowned interviewer. Under the stage lights, and surrounded by cameramen as well as a live audience, I knew that every word I spoke and gesture I made would be observed by millions of TV viewers. The stakes for my career were huge. So were the stakes for Procter & Gamble.

At thirty-six, I was now a senior researcher with P&G. My bosses had chosen me to go on *Oprah* and defend a new fat substitute called olestra. Olestra could be used in many kinds of foods and would not stay in the body, thus giving snacks the taste people crave while at the same time providing no calories from fat. Obviously, olestra held immense financial potential for the company. But there was a problem.

Just when P&G was seeking FDA approval of olestra for use in salty snacks like potato chips, a vocal critic arose. Michael Jacobson, executive director of the consumer advocacy group Center for Science in the Public Interest, seized on the possible digestive effects of olestra to wage a media war against it. During our test marketing in Columbus, Ohio, he announced, "Columbus is about to become the diarrhea capital of the world."[1] He implied—without evidence—that olestra could kill someone.[2]

Jacobson's attacks were successful in raising doubts about olestra's safety and also raised his profile in the public eye. And guess who Oprah invited to sit next to me on her show? Jacobson and I were going to be locked in a public relations showdown on the most popular TV show in America.

At this point I had worked as a scientist at P&G for ten years. What made me unusual, though, was that I also developed a knack for marketing and public relations. I had followed in the footsteps of my heroes Jacques Cousteau and Jane Goodall in making scientific topics understandable to a nonscientific audience. After years of explaining the science behind P&G's products to regulatory agencies in the United States and abroad, I was picked to represent the company in more public roles—in this case, defending olestra on *Oprah*. But for something as big as *Oprah*, I knew I needed help.

I worked with Cindy DiBiasi, a speaker trainer, for days prior to the episode's taping. Cindy and I studied past interviews on *Oprah* and worked on a game plan that would allow me to effectively communicate the facts about olestra while also winning over the crowd, which seemed primed to side with the consumer advocate over the big corporation.

I practiced and practiced. My emotions at the time alternated between confidence in our strategy and fear of being responsible for a high-profile failure.

In my hotel room in Chicago, before heading over to the station where the show would be taped, I got on my knees beside my bed and prayed. While I've always believed in God, I rarely prayed on my knees. But this time, I wanted God to see how serious the situation was. My prayers at that point in my life consisted entirely of requests for things I wanted from God—it was all about getting *him* to line up behind *my* plans—and this time was no different. I begged God to help me stick to the strategy and "win" the interview.

So now here I was, on the *Oprah* stage, with Michael Jacobson by my side and the great Oprah Winfrey standing in front of the audience, all ready to go for our segment.

With the cameras rolling, I explained what olestra was made of and how it reduced fat and calories in the diet.

Oprah was holding a snack-size bag of chips made with olestra. "In a small bag of potato chips like the one you have," I told Oprah, "you cut out ten grams of fat."

"*Mm-hmm*," Oprah said, skepticism in her voice. "But am I going to keel over and die later on?"

The audience laughed on cue.

"Absolutely not," I replied, smiling.

I delivered my carefully prepared line about olestra being "the most thoroughly researched and tested food ingredient ever. Period." Which to the best of my knowledge it was.

Next, Jacobson made his claims that olestra created gastric discomfort, stripped vitamins from the body, and might even cause cancer and blindness. His claims grossly exceeded the research evidence on the product. Whenever he said something unreliable, I shook my head or jumped in with a rebuttal.

Jacobson's demeanor quickly became sour and argumentative. Oprah let me interrupt him several times when he made outlandish statements because it made for good TV. At one point, Jacobson became frustrated and hit me on the arm. He seemed like a sore loser, which didn't help his case in the eyes of the audience.

One of the keys to my strategy was getting Oprah to taste the olestra chips during the show. This could change the debate away from diarrhea and nutritional apocalypse to a great-tasting, fat-free potato chip. While the show director was against the idea of giving Oprah chips with a controversial ingredient that hadn't yet been FDA approved, I convinced her to let Oprah decide for herself.

So this was the moment of truth. I asked Oprah to be the judge. "Try the chips."

She did. "I think they're really good!" she told the audience.

Before I knew it, the debate was over. Oprah ended the segment by saying the FDA would soon decide.

A few weeks later, on the morning of January 24, 1996, I was cooking pancakes in olestra when I received a call telling me the FDA would announce the approval of olestra later in the day. As far as the government go-ahead was concerned, we'd won! I drove to P&G headquarters in downtown Cincinnati to prepare for the media blitz I knew was about to start.

The *Oprah* interview I recorded aired that same afternoon. P&G leadership was ecstatic about both the governmental approval and the *Oprah* interview. Charlotte Otto, the head of public relations, and John Pepper, P&G's CEO, both called to congratulate me.

I was flying high. I believed this product would be a big hit and I would ride its success to even greater things. It never crossed my mind that the God I was functionally ignoring at the time might have already set in motion a different plan for me.

With my successful appearance on the *Oprah* show and the FDA's approval of olestra, I thought opposition would soon die down and I could be part of a major success. The real outcome was different. Instead of dying down, the controversy over olestra became the most visible and longest-lasting of any media storm P&G had ever experienced.

I was now the go-to P&G spokesperson for almost every olestra-related interview. I spent weeks in our test markets around the country. I developed a network of supportive gastroenterologists and dietitians in each market, and Cindy DiBiasi and I trained them how to respond to the media. When it came time for the national launch of olestra in 1998, I identified and trained dietitians in every major media market nationwide.

With extensive studies on larger numbers of people, the gastrointestinal and nutritional safety of olestra continued to be confirmed.[3] Yet the FDA initially required an informational label on the product about potential gastrointestinal and nutrition effects. This reinforced Jacobson's criticism, and he was able to continue his campaign beyond our national launch.

During this period, P&G worked with some high-profile scientists, including Dr. Louis Sullivan, former secretary of Health and Human Services. I asked Dr. Sullivan about the attacks on olestra. "Is P&G doing the right thing?"

"Greg," he told me, "you will know you are doing disruptive work when you are under attack. P&G is doing the right thing." This response was helpful in the moment and is an insight I've often returned to.

For several years, P&G continued the fight. FritoLay launched olestra versions of their best-selling potato chips and tortilla chips (Lay's, Ruffles, Doritos), and P&G's own Pringles brand brought out a fat-free version with olestra. These products were among the top new product entries in the late 1990s. Unfortunately, the product did not meet P&G's high expectations of consumer appeal and sales. Given the high costs of the many studies P&G funded to establish the safety of the product, the lower-than-expected sales led to a deep financial hole, and by 2002 the company made the decision to write off the loss.

While some products that contain olestra are still on the market, it's fair to say olestra was a financial failure. It took decades of research and never made a profit. I believe we got the science right, but we lost in the eyes of the public.

As olestra wound toward its sad end, I took on several other assignments at P&G, and these led to commercial failures of their own. The products included the drink mix NutriStar and an ill-fated joint venture with Coca-Cola. At the time, it was devastating to work on failure after failure, even though I knew that with each setback I was learning new skills that could later be essential in other work.

I had started my career with such hope and promise, and here I was, feeling like I was tagged with failure. I was disappointed, embarrassed, and bitter about it for years afterward.

By the spring of 2000, I thought my time at P&G might be drawing to a close, and I was looking for other job opportunities. But before anything serious materialized, Charlotte Otto asked me to meet with her in her office.

Charlotte was an elegant, no-nonsense woman. She'd known me since I'd jumped into the olestra media maelstrom. When I arrived at her office, she got right down to business. "I want you to move to the personal health care division and lead the efforts to build external support for those products." I knew the major personal care lines included old standards Pepto-Bismol, Vicks, and Metamucil, along with some products we were working to bring to market, including the heat wrap ThermaCare and the heartburn drug Prilosec OTC.

This wasn't the first time Charlotte had offered me a job. I'd turned her down before, saying I didn't want to do *only* public relations. I liked having a job that included scientific work.

But before I could turn her down this time, she played her trump card. "There's also a water purification product," she said. "It's part of the division you'd be joining. It's honestly amazing. Simply new to the world."

This was news to me. "What do you mean?" I asked. "Tell me about it."

"It's a packet that cleans and purifies water—even dirty water." Then she interrupted herself. "I'll tell you what, why don't you go to the lab where they're working on it and ask *them* about it? Then give me your answer on the new job."

As Charlotte had foreseen, I was intrigued. Later that week I was in my car, driving to the P&G labs outside Cincinnati to see this water miracle for myself.

3

MAGIC IN A PACKET

Carrying the bucket I used to mop the floors, I walked down the slope to the lightly wooded creek behind my house in suburban Cincinnati and filled the bucket with water. This was spring runoff time, and the water was quite dirty and probably filled with parasites and who knows what other biologicals.

By this time, I was married and had two daughters, Ashton and Meredith. My wife's grandfather, Buddy, who was also raised in North Carolina, was visiting us, and he joined me in the kitchen as I poured a packet of Procter & Gamble's experimental water purification powder into the dirty water. Then I took a wooden spoon and started the prescribed five minutes of stirring. While we waited for the chemicals to begin working, Buddy told me stories of fetching water from a well when he was growing up on a farm. I told him about my great-grandmother who had died from a waterborne disease, probably cholera. It was amazing to think that, if this packet worked, it could have saved her life.

In the swirl of water, we could soon see the dirt gathering in larger and larger clumps. After five minutes, all the visible material had sunk to the bottom. I carefully strained the water through a cloth, and it looked as pure as tap water. We waited the required twenty minutes for the water to be fully disinfected, and then I poured Buddy and myself glassfuls. We looked at each other doubtfully. But with only a moment's hesitation, we clinked glasses and drank.

I was astonished.

The packet had worked. What had started out as dirty creek water was now as clean as water from the tap.

This transformation seemed like magic. But it wasn't magic. It was science.

As I'd discovered in my visit to the P&G laboratories, scientist Phil Souter had figured out a way to combine the same chemicals municipal water treatment plants use but in such a way as to treat small quantities of water. Each tea-bag-size packet contained enough powder to purify ten liters of even extremely filthy water. The powder ingredients included a coagulant and a flocculant effective in removing dirt, worms, and parasites. They also included a chlorine disinfectant to kill bacteria and viruses.

This stuff turned dangerous water into purified drinking water, and *you could actually see it happening*. The scientist in me was impressed. The marketer in me was imagining the possibilities. I felt the skills I'd honed on my previous assignments could take this packet and change millions of lives forever.

Charlotte Otto had offered me a new job within P&G. The water effort would be a small part of my overall responsibilities, but it was the part that got me excited. I called Charlotte. "I'll take it," I told her.

Not long after I joined the personal health care division, P&G acquired the PUR water filtration business. The PUR name was a great fit, so the packets took the name PUR Purifier of Water.

My role in the P&G global water effort was to develop the strategy and execute efforts to build support for the water purification packets. A big task for our team at first was international test marketing, involving experiments in how to get the packets to people who could use them and collecting and analyzing data on how people reacted to them. We recognized that the packets would be needed only in places where safe drinking water is not reliably available, so we planned to test market them first in Guatemala in 2000, then in Morocco, the Philippines, and Pakistan over the next four years. These were all countries where P&G already had a footprint.

Initially I thought we could have a big brand on our hands, even though most of our users would be the world's poorest people.[1] Because we planned to sell the packets at a price our users could afford, we would need to see high adoption rates in the countries where we had a presence in the developing world. The test marketing was crucial to determine whether we could reach our targets.

At the same time I was trying to establish the product's commercial viability, I had the equally important task of building support for the product within the company.

I enlisted the help of Cindy DiBiasi—the speaker trainer who helped me prepare for *Oprah*, who had since started her own communications company—and we created a video showcasing P&G's water work in Guatemala. We recorded a mother gathering water from a spring, carrying it back to her home in a plastic jug, and then using the P&G packets to purify the water. We also interviewed a nurse talking about the prevalence of diarrheal disease and how the packets could help. I narrated the video and talked about the power of the packets.

I spent many hours editing the video to show exactly what I hoped to share. I believed it captured the beauty of the Indigenous people of Guatemala, their struggles with unclean water, and the magic of the P&G packets in turning contaminated water into potable water.

Viewing the video, Bob Greene, our head of research and development within personal health care, quickly got the connection between the packets and P&G's values of improving the lives of consumers and always trying to do the right thing.

"Let's show it to John," Bob said.

John Pepper was a former CEO of P&G. He had retired a couple of years earlier, but to many of us he was still the closest thing to a living embodiment of the company. Under John's leadership, P&G had defined its principles, values, and purpose, and so in a way John's sterling character had entered the DNA of the company.[2]

I liked and even revered John, and he had taken an interest in my career since the olestra days. To me, John's reaction to the video would tell us whether we were on the right track.

Still relatively young at the time, John had dark hair, a broad smile, and a warm personality. It was great to see him again for the video presentation, held in one of the company's meeting rooms. After so many hours of watching the same video, you'd think it would get stale to me. But watching the video with John Pepper, the person who, to me, best represented the heart and soul of P&G, created an almost sacred space. I was glad we had turned out the lights because it concealed the tears that came to my eyes as the video went on. But I needn't have been self-conscious. As we turned the lights back up, I could see that John, Bob, and my boss, Don Tassone, were also crying. Tears at a corporate meeting! That was a first for me, and honestly it shocked me.

John didn't say much after the video. He didn't have to. It was obvious it had touched him as much as it had the rest of us. And if we were able to touch *his* heart, then it was clear we could do the same with others. The packets had the potential to make the purpose of the company come to life.

"Thank you for showing me this," John said. "This is critical work. Keep me updated, and let me know if there's anything I can do to help."

Up until that time, the scales of my career had tilted more toward failure than success. With John's blessing on the water project, I felt I needed to make sure that this time we succeeded.

At the same time, of course, I was still working with other products. One was a digestive health product that was about to be the source of controversy.

I was headed to the airport on a Friday afternoon in January 2003 when I received an urgent call from one of our personal health care brand managers. "You're not going to believe this," he said, "but we got a call from a *New York Times* reporter. Apparently, the superintendent of Yellowstone National Park is upset at us, and the reporter needs a statement from us right away if we want to get it in before the story runs."

I almost laughed. "Why?"

It turns out the *New York Times* reporter had gone to Yellowstone to do a story about the bison, but all the superintendent wanted to talk about was our new commercial. I hadn't seen it. "Can you play it for me over the phone so I know what we're dealing with?" I asked. (This was prior to smartphones, so I couldn't pull up a video myself.)

In the ad, a Yellowstone ranger is standing in front of Old Faithful geyser, talking to a group of tourists. "Every day for thousands of years Old Faithful has been, well, faithful. You can almost set your watch by it."

A woman in the group raises her hand and asks, "What causes it to stay so regular?"

The ad flashes back to a ranger pouring our product into the geyser and concludes with the geyser erupting.

I could guess what the controversy was about. "I'll bet the superintendent is concerned about people messing with geysers," I told the brand manager. "I'll call the reporter right away."

I had to develop my game plan while driving to the airport. Instead of saying that we take all concerns seriously and promising to investigate—which would be the expected corporate line—I decided to go for a more logical approach. Let's face it: The ad was clever and funny. Why not reinforce that?

I called Katharine Seelye of the *Times*. "I'm Dr. Greg Allgood of the P&G Health Sciences Institute," I said, "and I understand you want to talk about our new ad."

"Yes, that's right," she said.

"Can you tell me what this is about? I don't have any further details."

I had been right about the reason for the Yellowstone superintendent's anger at P&G. As she explained it, the Yellowstone superintendent didn't want the ad to encourage people to cross safety lines at the geysers.

"You're kidding!" I said. "We thought the commercial was so over the top that everyone would laugh. Clearly when you try humor, not everyone gets it."

And this was how I was quoted in the *Times* in a story that was favorable to P&G.[3] Yet what really got the reporter on our side, I think, was what I said next.

"Actually, my doctoral thesis examined the effects of oxygen on the thermophilic bacteria found at Old Faithful."

"Really?" I could hear skepticism in her voice. She had called P&G late on a Friday before a holiday weekend, expecting to talk to someone in corporate communications, and instead she got a spokesperson who did research on bacteria from Yellowstone? "Tell me about your research," she said.

I launched into technical details about how thermophilic bacteria may have been some of the first life to develop on earth. After a few minutes, I said, "I'm glad you're interested in my doctoral research! Most people get bored when I explain it."

Taking our conversation full circle, I added, "I love Yellowstone and Old Faithful. I've been out there several times and never thought the commercial would encourage people to damage Old Faithful." Katharine also included this in her article.

I was successful in getting P&G out of hot water (pun intended) but didn't expect what happened next. Popular radio show hosts who had seen the *Times* article, including Mitch Albom, invited me as a guest on their shows as they bashed the National Park Service for having no sense of humor. It went too far, and I was worried about long-term damage to the people who serve in the National Park Service.

At my request, P&G put a disclaimer on the commercial that read "Dramatization—Please Obey Park Service Rules." I also apologized to the leadership at the National Park Service for the way this had spun out. They were overjoyed to put this behind them.

It had turned out well for us too. Brand sales increased, and I like to think that my efforts with the *Times* and the addition of the TV disclaimer were part of the success.

Looking back, I'm proud that my doctoral research helped lead to a commercial win in my career. I'm less proud that my pride and presumption led me to achieve a publicity success through making fun of the National Park Service. In a way, I'd become what I'd feared when I first turned down work with P&G's public relations division after *Oprah*—I'd become a corporate spokesperson not really doing science.

This was why I was eager to continue work on the water purification packets. My work with the packets also involved promotion, but for me it tapped into purpose in a much deeper way. As the test marketing went on, I spent significant time in the developing world, visiting people in their homes and learning from them about their lives and their use of the packets. This was when I met Mercy and learned her story. While I'd seen poverty before, this was a deeper experience, and it solidified my resolve to pursue solutions to the global water crisis.

I didn't suspect that my newfound resolve would soon be put to the test.

4

TESTING THE WATERS

The heartburn medicine Prilosec was the biggest-selling prescription drug in the world. In 2003, as we sought to get FDA approval to sell Prilosec over the counter, I was responsible for the public relations work, drafting and refining our messaging, getting our thought leaders ready, and responding to the media. It was a thrill when we learned that on June 20, the FDA was going to grant its approval. We would make a major announcement about this milestone from our international headquarters in Cincinnati, launching the product.

Clearly, my place on June 20 was at the Prilosec OTC announcement, assisting with the media interviews. There was just one hitch. We had already scheduled the launch of the PUR Purifier of Water packets for the exact same day—in London.

Prilosec was a top-selling prescription drug, so hopes were high for the over-the-counter version. In contrast, making a successful business from the packets was going to be a huge challenge because of the difficulties in accessing developing-world markets and changing people's habits to treat their water before use. Given my past experiences with product launches that did not result in successful businesses, I should have devoted more effort to Prilosec. But my heart was with the product that could potentially help address the global water crisis. With the two launches occurring on the same day, I chose to be present for the London launch of the packets.

Actually, I was determined to pull off my media relations duties for *both* launches. I worked furiously out of New York City with our public relations agency for Prilosec and then took an overnight flight to London for the water packets' launch. From London, I could continue to respond to US media queries following the FDA announcement about Prilosec. My passion to make sure the packets succeeded drove my decision to participate in both launches on the same day.

That's how, on the morning of June 20, I found myself walking down Parliament Street from Trafalgar Square toward Big Ben and past 10 Downing Street. With me were Stephen Luby of the US Centers for Disease Control (CDC) and Linda Carrier-Walker of the International Council of Nurses. We were heading to a press conference at the Royal Academy of Engineering near St. James's Park. I was jet-lagged and exhausted, having barely slept the night before. But mostly, as we walked those famous London streets, I felt a profound sense of contentment. My company would now officially be in the business of selling the water purification packets.

The fact that we were making the PUR packets announcement in London communicated that this would be a global product. Having representatives from two of our important partners in government and nursing demonstrated that our campaign was a collaborative effort with important health consequences. Journalists were on hand as one of our UK managers read the official press release explaining how the packets had the potential to reduce disease prevalence and transform lives among some of the most at-risk populations in the world.[1]

As I listened, I told myself I was going to be a part of a meaningful success and put olestra and other failures behind me. But could we really make it work?

I had done a lot of research to determine how we might structure the PUR packets business. I gained agreement to a three-pronged strategy consisting of (1) seeking commercial success in individual countries in the developing world where Procter & Gamble had good infrastructure, which included much of Latin America, the Middle East, many countries in Asia, and a handful of African countries; (2) providing the product at cost for use in emergencies by groups like UNICEF; and (3) letting other groups distribute the product in countries where P&G had no presence, like Haiti and Uganda.

It wasn't difficult to get people on board with providing the product free of charge during emergencies. P&G had been making product donations during emergencies for decades. My challenge in this area was to communicate that we *needed* to charge for the product versus donating it. Because the demand in an emergency would likely be huge, we needed to cover our costs to keep production sustainable. However, I knew P&G also had a grant-making fund that could help to cover costs for the transportation and training needed for those who couldn't afford these costs in an immediate emergency.

For the third approach—providing the product to other groups in countries where P&G had little or no presence—I helped our leaders understand that if we achieved success in areas with P&G infrastructure, there would be increasing pressure to provide the product in areas where we did not have distribution. The challenges faced by pharmaceutical companies with antiretroviral drugs to treat HIV/AIDS, which led to demand for generic versions and lower-cost drugs, was a good illustration. We needed to have a plan to provide the product globally, even in areas P&G was not currently reaching. But how would we do this?

In my discussions with the CDC, I learned about PSI, a nongovernmental organization (NGO) that was a global leader in social marketing. Social marketing is an approach that uses marketing principles and concepts to provide products and services contributing to social good. In other words, PSI was an NGO who sold products in the developing world. For example, they were already selling a simple chlorine disinfectant for water treatment called WaterGuard. They used methods familiar to P&G of product and packaging design, pricing, placement, and promotion, including mass advertising. PSI's footprint was strong in the developing world where P&G had no presence.

Even though P&G leadership could easily understand how PSI might be successful with the packets, there was reluctance to give up too much control over one of our products. My breakthrough in gaining acceptance came about when P&G's treasurer at the time, John Goodwin, agreed to meet with PSI and then went to see their work in Uganda. After digging into PSI's approach and finances, John assured P&G senior leadership that we had done our due diligence.

With John's endorsement of PSI, P&G agreed to the three-pronged strategy. I was part of a global team of more than twenty people, including some of our best and most dedicated marketers, pursuing the commercial strategy. Emergency and social marketing were entirely up to me.

I felt enormous pressure at this point in my career from the workload and because our test markets with the packets were not meeting our sales expectations due to the difficulty of changing people's habits to treat their drinking water. Because of this, we had recently closed the test market in Guatemala.

We had a smart and dedicated team in Guatemala collaborating with our US staff and partner Johns Hopkins University. We were learning a tremendous amount about marketing the packets to people in extreme poverty. Based on work with consumers, we learned the packets had to be the price of an everyday item that even people in poverty could typically afford. We set the price of the packets at one quetzal, the price of a single egg and at the time equivalent to a dime in the United States. This price pushed our product supply team to get the cost down, and eventually they delivered.

Our Johns Hopkins partners had told us we were setting a high bar in starting our test markets in Guatemala. They knew habit change among the Indigenous Mayan population was difficult. Our team in Guatemala worked harder than any team I'd ever been associated with, but the Johns Hopkins people were right—our expectations were just too high.

After the Guatemala test market closed, we entered Morocco and the Philippines with the packets. Our test markets in these places were micro-test markets so we could gain information quickly and adapt without huge investments. We found that we couldn't get people to keep purchasing the packets at high enough levels, even after extensive marketing on radio and television. Many on our team still believed we just needed to find the right message to convince them. But others, including myself, believed our product wasn't the best option for most people.

I held this opinion because the magic of the P&G packets shows up when it turns *visibly* dirty water clean, as happened at Mercy's pond in Kenya. Seeing is believing, and the dramatic impact of this miraculous cleaning only happens when the water looks initially dirty. In our test markets, most people were drinking contaminated water, but the water *appeared* to be clear. Without the magic moment, the stirring and filtering were a lot to ask someone to do.

The opinion that we could develop a market among people

drinking clean but contaminated water was based on a belief that we could help people understand that clean-looking water isn't necessarily safe water. We focused our educational and marketing efforts to help people understand this.

But again, we were not able to sustain the needed level of sales and closed the test markets in the Philippines and Morocco before moving on to Pakistan, where the rate of illness from unsafe water was high.

It was at this point that my failures started to weigh on me. There was the reality of three test markets we had closed without meeting expectations, even if two of them were low-cost efforts in micro markets. The cost of development and test marketing was coming to a point that it seemed unlikely we could reach profitability with the packets.

I was the only one on our team acknowledging these facts. P&G people are high-performing and incredibly determined. They frequently turn around businesses that are struggling. The mindset was to keep at it—to work harder and more creatively. No one on the team was willing to talk to me about a backup plan.

I decided it was up to me to create an alternative for success.

When looking at our three-pronged strategy of commercial success, emergency relief, and social marketing, I was beginning to believe we should continue the emergency relief and social-marketing efforts even if the P&G commercial approach failed. This was a radical idea. It would mean P&G agreeing to run a not-for-profit business. The company had not done anything like this in its entire 180-year history.

Other for-profit companies had successfully used nonprofit strategies to distribute products to people who desperately needed them. The most relevant example was pharmaceutical giant Merck's donation program for Mectizan—a product that treats river blindness and lymphatic filariasis. Merck's donation program now treats three hundred million people annually, with more than four billion treatments donated since 1987. Numerous countries have *eliminated* river blindness or lymphatic filariasis as a result.[2] But even in that case there was a big difference because a person needs only an annual dose of Mectizan, whereas people need clean water every day. At P&G this kind of nonprofit approach for the water purifier was a disruptive idea, and I knew I might have a hard time selling it internally. Still, I thought the strategy could work. Although it wouldn't add to the company's bottom line, it was in keeping with our values and would create goodwill for the company.

Not that I really wanted to be involved in a nonprofit organization. I wanted to be involved in business. From the time I was in college, I had been reading management books like *The One Minute Manager* by Ken Blanchard. I wanted to become well-known in the corporate world. Honestly, I tended to look down on nonprofits. At the time I thought nonprofits couldn't possibly have sufficient enough resources to hire the best talent or make the greatest impact. So switching to a nonprofit model would be a big adjustment for me, personally, as much as it would be for my company. And yet if I was going to help people like Mercy with the water purification packets, it was looking like we had to do it without the commercial component.

How would I promote my nonprofit strategy? I needed allies.

And I knew there was only one option: a one-page memo.

P&G is famous for the one-page memo. Multimillion-dollar decisions have been made based on the rationale shared succinctly in a one-pager. Writing this kind of document demands special communication skills, and all P&G managers are trained in this discipline. I could write a one-page recommendation summarizing the broad value to P&G of continuing the packets effort even if they failed commercially.

Here's the catch. The P&G memo starts with the recommendation of action. It's like switching the conclusion from the bottom of the page to the top so a reader knows exactly where you're going from the start. My recommendation of action would be that, even if we could not create a commercially viable product, we should continue to distribute the packets through social marketing and emergency relief as a nonprofit business within the corporation. My problem was that my team, at this point, was unwilling to admit potential failure of the commercial effort. If I wrote a one-page memo in the usual way, it would be a nonstarter from the first sentence.

So to promote my nontraditional strategy, I wrote a nontraditional memo. I drafted the memo without a clear recommendation, though I knew I would eventually need to make that addition. At this point I remained vague as I started a conversation using the memo as a tool to gain support from key allies. Some people thought I needed to be sent back to P&G memo-writing school for not including a recommendation, but it was the only option for the catch-22 I was facing.

Over a period of a few months, I developed my nonprofit strategy and shared my memo with people like Charlotte Otto (head of external relations), George Carpenter (leader of P&G's sustainability group), Paul Polman (leader of P&G Europe and a champion of our sustainability efforts), and Carolyn Brehm (P&G government relations). I got qualified support or at least a show of interest from each of them.

It was toward the end of this time that I went back to Kenya to check on the status of a small pilot of the social-marketing model.

5

STOPPED IN MY TRACKS

By the fall of 2004, HIV/AIDS was ravaging many parts of Africa. The stigma was so great that it was sometimes hard to get people talking about the disease and how to help its victims and prevent further spread. This was also prior to the widespread distribution of antiretroviral drugs to prevent the progression of AIDS. The toll on life in sub-Saharan Africa was horrific, with one person dying from AIDS-related disease every fifteen seconds.

One of the primary causes of death among people living with AIDS was diarrhea caused by drinking contaminated water. This fact wasn't well accepted at the time by the public health community, at least not to an extent that many were reaching out to people living with AIDS to make sure they had clean water.

In Kenya, women's groups were selling a low-cost chlorine solution for disinfecting water, but the simple disinfectants were not able to remove parasites. These parasites could cause infections that, though possibly mild in healthy adults, could be fatal in people with AIDS. And so, about a year earlier, I had teamed up with staff from the CDC to provide packets left over from our clinical study to one of the women's groups selling the chlorine. Now I wanted to see the results.

To reach my destination, I traveled bumpy roads in a Land Cruiser with Alie Eleveld, a Dutch woman with a big heart who worked with an organization called Safe Water and AIDS Project (SWAP). She took me to a rural village in far western Kenya. This was an area where ponds dug into the red-clay landscape served as the water source for cows, goats, sheep, chickens, dogs, *and* people. In other words, they were exactly the sort of ponds that harbor dangerous parasites.

A couple of years earlier, I had met Mercy and her two children in a similar setting in another part of Kenya, and that's when I had fully understood the importance of the safe water program I had joined. Since then, the road to getting Procter & Gamble's safe drinking water program going had been as bumpy as the roads Alie and I had taken to get to this village. But now I was about to meet another woman who would recharge my motivation.

Alie brought me to meet Jemima (pronounced juh-MEEM-uh) Odo. Jemima was in her late forties at the time, married to James, and had several children and grandchildren.[1] The couple lived in a mud hut with a thatch roof.

Looking out the window of our vehicle as we drove up, we saw Jemima sweeping in front of her hut, using a homemade broom constructed of a stick with leaves tied on the end. She was sweeping away debris and chicken droppings to make a tidy place for us to visit.

When Jemima spotted us, she didn't wait for us to come to her but ran to our vehicle to greet us. She was thin, and her clothes were ragged but clean. She had a wonderful smile and, despite how frail she was, seemed full of life.

She gave Alie—an old friend of hers—a long hug. Then to my

surprise she did the same to me. She took me by the hand and led me to a hand-carved wooden stool in front of her hut and invited me to sit.

In her heavily accented English, Jemima told me her story. She shared that she had acquired HIV and it had progressed to having AIDS health symptoms. She'd had persistent and severe diarrhea, and her weight had dropped to seventy pounds. "I was no longer able to walk to the pond for water," she told us. "My daughter Caroline had to do all the hauling for my family." Jemima's health continued to decline, and she became bedridden. "I thought I was going to die."

Jemima's story broke my heart, especially because I knew she represented so many others.

She continued, "But then my family received the packets. We cleaned our water every day. And my health started to improve."

Her amazing spirit shone through as she described her remarkable health comeback over the past year. "This product saved my life," she declared.

I knew the P&G packets could help people, but it still took me aback to see the results up close.

Jemima told me, "I now teach AIDS prevention and empowerment for girls." She was helping to erase the stigma against AIDS testing by being tested herself and by publicly announcing she had AIDS. Following her example, more than eight hundred fellow villagers had been tested. She was caring for thirty AIDS orphans, including nine of her own grandchildren. She was also now selling the P&G water purification packets, using the profit to support her growing family.

Proudly, she said, "I am one of the leading sales agents of the packets in this area."

Before we left, Jemima took me by the hand again and leaned toward me. "Tell people my story. People here are dying from diarrhea, and they need these packets."

As Alie and I walked back to the vehicle, my emotions welled up inside of me. Meeting Mercy had made me determined to get to work on the water purification project, but somehow meeting Jemima was far more moving for me. I kept my composure until we were out of sight of Jemima's hut, and then I wept. I'd just been told a Lazarus-like story of someone who had almost died but then recovered. I wept because I was all too aware of my own track record of failures. I was distraught at the possibility of not being able to help more people like Jemima.[2]

Did I have as much courage and determination as Jemima did for the challenges lying before me?

Back at P&G, the leaders of the personal health care division convened an emergency meeting. The test marketing of the water purification packets was going poorly. I was part of the leadership team, but the others deliberately did not include me in the meeting invitation. Our vice president told the team I was too emotionally involved in the project. The decision reached in the meeting was to disband the global water purification team. The test marketing would continue in Pakistan with only our Pakistani staff, to see if they could pull off a turnaround. Otherwise, there would be no more investment in the project.

I was called into our vice president's office to hear the news firsthand. "You're no longer responsible for the packets," he told me. "You're doing a great job on leading the external relations work for our other brands, but as for the water purification program . . ."

I was out.

"I don't want you to feel too badly about this, Greg," he continued. "I know you've worked hard for the water packets. But we have to be realistic. The test-marketing results to date have been discouraging enough that the company has serious doubts about the commercial viability of this product."

"What if you kept just me working on this project?" I asked. "Let me see what I can do."

He shook his head. "A lot of bright people were involved in trying to make this product profitable, and they failed. You couldn't run it yourself. You're not even a marketer. You're a scientist."

This looked like the end. Even though I had seen it coming, I wasn't emotionally prepared for it. I was devastated. Yet again I was facing failure.

But I remembered Jemima's courage. She was so committed to sharing the packets, and I couldn't let her down. I knew I had to do what I could to keep the effort going.

The next day I asked to meet again with our vice president, and this time I brought my boss, Don Tassone. Knowing the financial pressures that led to disbanding the team, we acknowledged it was necessary to remove any loss from the personal health care division. "The broad benefit of this effort, and thus the cost, should be shouldered by the entire company," we argued.

Earlier I had shared with this VP my idea about dropping the commercial part of the three-pronged strategy and keeping the emergency and social marketing parts in place, with me running them on my own. Now Don and I raised this idea again.

"Could you give us six months to fully develop a plan to continue with the social marketing and emergency efforts?" Don asked.

"You have one month," the VP countered.

We got to work.

A single month should have been impossible, and I suspect our vice president knew this. But he didn't know I'd already rounded up support from some of our corporate leaders for my one-page recommendation. Now I added the top-line recommendation and tried to gain full support for the idea.

Then several people, all of whom I trusted and had great respect for, told me that the vice president was planning to end my career with P&G.

My heart dropped.

The VP's reason for wanting to fire me was the disruptive nature of my plans to create a nonprofit unit within P&G. His concern about the risk to P&G's reputation was legitimate. The PUR Purifier of Water packets had the same name as our PUR Water Filtration business, and confusion about the lack of commercial success with the packets would likely spill over to our growing filtration business. There was also a broader risk to all of P&G for continuing to push a product that test markets had clearly shown did not have sufficient consumer appeal.

As much as hearing this hurt, I had to agree these were excellent points. But why go so far as to have me fired? I'd developed a deserved reputation as a fighter even back in the days of olestra, when they'd picked me to debate Michael Jacobson on *Oprah*. I was viewed as relentless as a bulldog, and I couldn't disagree.

It's also true that in a corporation there needs to be a way to stop people from pursuing their own pet projects. If they pursue their own agenda and don't align with the agreed strategy, then businesses fail. So even though I was in the crosshairs, I could see the wisdom in what the VP was doing.

Still, I felt like I was just starting to run in my purpose to bring clean water to people who needed it, and now I was about to be stopped in my tracks. I was in a panic and didn't know what to do.

I remembered the words Dr. Louis Sullivan had given me during the olestra days: "You will know you are doing disruptive work when you are under attack." What I was doing *was* disruptive, and I *was* under attack. And just as I did then, I believed I was doing the right thing.

I was scheduled to go to Geneva, Switzerland, to attend a meeting of P&G's global corporate sustainability team. The team was led by George Carpenter, who had said he wanted to brainstorm how his team could support my memo's recommendation. Even with my employment at P&G hanging by a thread, it seemed like it could still be worthwhile to attend this meeting. If nothing else, it would give me a chance to get away and gain a new perspective on my situation.

I made the trip to Geneva in October 2004, bringing my panic with me. On the first morning of my visit, I went for a run beside Lake Geneva to try to relax.

I'd been to Geneva many times because it was the headquarters of the World Health Organization. It is a beautiful place to run, with the water reflecting the Alps in the distance. You can glance up at the steeple of St. Peter's Cathedral in the old city or watch water erupt from the water cannon in the bay. This was a quiet, lovely day, with blue skies and calm water. But as tranquil as the setting was, I was feeling anything but tranquil.

The pressure inside me was immense. Thoughts of what I should do kept rolling around in my mind. If I continued pushing for P&G to maintain its safe water campaign in a nonprofit way, I would likely lose my job. Even though most of my career had been associated with commercial failures, getting fired felt deeply personal. It would create a financial hit for my family at a time when we had just moved into a new and larger house, and I had already sacrificed a good deal to get this program off the ground. Losing my job would disrupt our lives even more. I told myself I needed to stop—to give up on this crazy idea and resume my work with other brands. Besides, I was sure there would be other meaningful assignments if I stayed with P&G.

On the other hand, did I really want to quit on something that was so important and that gave me such a sense of purpose? But also, was there any hope for the nonprofit plan?

I struggled through the first half of my run. Usually by this point in the workout, the physical exertion would have begun alleviating my stress. This time, though, the stress inside me was still mounting. I could feel my heart pounding from anxiety as much as from the run. I felt like I couldn't get enough air into my lungs even though I wasn't running particularly fast.

Then I heard a voice speak to me. It stopped me in my tracks.

Nobody was near me. I knew this was God. He said, *Do you doubt I can do this?*

Exactly those words. As plain as the Alpine sunshine.

I'd always been a person of faith, but more the "frozen chosen" kind of Christian. I believed in God, but we weren't usually on speaking terms unless there was a crisis, and then I usually did the talking. Having God speak to me was completely unlike any experience of my life. Yet there was no doubt I had heard God speak this time.

I fell to my knees, still sensing I was in God's presence. Tears ran down my face. *What does this mean?*

I repeated the words God had given me. *Do you doubt I can do this?* I believed God was saying he would enable me to pull off the nonprofit water strategy I had devised.

And the answer was that I did *not* doubt this. I was convinced God could make the program succeed against all the odds I was facing.

I cried, shaking, still on my knees, for several minutes.

The cool air from Lake Geneva combined with my sweaty shirt from the run had me shivering. I finally stood up and walked back to my hotel. As the shock of the experience left me, I felt changed.

The fear and doubt were gone. My past failures melted away. With God's help, I would move forward.

6

GOING IT ALONE

After God said, *Do you doubt I can do this?* and brought me to my knees during my run beside Lake Geneva, I had to go to the meeting with George Carpenter and his sustainability team. They all knew about the shutdown of the water program and were agitated about the apparent loss of this opportunity for Procter & Gamble to help some of the world's neediest people.

I didn't say anything to them about how God had spoken to me. Being open about my faith like that would have been confusing. While many people at P&G have faith, of all different kinds, explicitly applying faith to corporate decisions is not generally accepted as a business strategy. And besides, at that point in my own spiritual development, I would have felt awkward talking about it.

But in a way, the experience spoke for itself. I *had* been changed. I was now certain of the water program's eventual success. Somehow

I was able to absorb the fears George and others were expressing and to exude confidence. My calm helped others grow calm.

Back home, though, I knew I'd have my work cut out for me. I had to get the company leaders to sign off on the nonprofit model.

My boss, Don Tassone, who reported to Charlotte Otto, was one of my strongest allies, but he tended to support me quietly and diplomatically so he could continue to have a seat at the table without seeming to represent a position. He could be in the rooms where I wasn't invited because of my passion. We talked about the status of the water project, and he confirmed that my job was on the line. Then he gave me a task.

"Greg, let's try something. I want you to write the story of what would happen if P&G makes this radical decision to continue the work. Write it as if from five years in the future."

I thought this was a great idea. I drafted a little story about how pursuing the nonprofit strategy for the packets aligned with our corporate purpose and how, through partnering with other organizations, we could efficiently target people who had visibly dirty water.

When Don had read the story, he called me into his office to discuss it. "I don't think you're reaching high enough," he told me. Since getting the program off the ground at all seemed a stretch, I thought I had done pretty well! But he reminded me, "P&G has never done something like this. You're seeking to increase corporate overhead at a time we're being asked to decrease. Try again—and think big."

In my new story of the future, I described how in five years we would celebrate providing the billionth liter of clean water, and John Pepper would come out of retirement to personally deliver it. I described further how P&G had been praised by presidents and kings for its efforts to provide clean water and had received many awards. In my vision, the safe drinking water efforts had brought the soul of the company to life, and it had brought in new business for P&G brands as well.

I shared this new version with Don.

"That's it!" he said.

I loved the ideas I'd written down, but even with the confidence I had from my Geneva experience, I wasn't sure I totally believed it would happen. And yet I know now that somehow God was giving me a vision of what he was actually going to do.

Because, in fact, *every word* of it would come true.

While dreaming about the future inspired me, I wanted a check on my rationale and requested a meeting with former P&G CEO John Pepper. Since showing him the video we'd filmed in Guatemala, I'd been keeping him updated on the water purification project. He knew about the disappointing results of the test markets and the decision to shut down the project. Now I wanted to talk to him about my idea to keep going with the nonprofit side of the work.

Since John didn't have an official role in the company anymore, I didn't want to ask him to get involved in the debate with the decision-makers. Still, I valued his opinion. I promised myself that if John Pepper thought my idea wasn't going to work, I'd pull back.

Like other former CEOs, John maintained an office at the P&G headquarters even in retirement, and that's where we had our meeting. As I described the global water crisis and our ideas about how we could help, I became quite animated. "These water purification packets bring our corporate purpose to life!" I practically shouted, pounding my fist on John's desk.

John sat back in his chair and looked at me.

I stopped talking. I realized I'd gone too far.

John said, "I don't get it."

Okay, I told myself, *get ready for some bad news.*

John repeated, "I don't get it. *Of course* the company will support this effort, because it's the right thing to do."

My relief must have been visible all over my face.

"This is critical work," he said, "and we need someone capable of leading it." He paused and smiled. "Maybe I'll come out of retirement to help."

I couldn't help smiling too. "That's an excellent idea, John!"

"I'm just kidding. *You* should lead this effort."

I thanked John for his time and encouragement. When I left his office, I was elated.

But John was our *former* CEO. I still needed to persuade our *current* CEO.

Charlotte Otto arranged a meeting with our CEO, A. G. Lafley, to be held on the eleventh floor of one of P&G's twin towers in downtown Cincinnati. The towers and surrounding two blocks of gardens are quite a show of corporate success. To get to the executive offices, you pass through a security area and enter a series of nicely appointed suites facing the view south toward the Ohio River. In the middle of the bank of suites is a big, round table easily reached from the executive offices.

I felt like I was about to sit at the famed Round Table of Camelot, except the roundness of *this* table didn't imply an equal sharing of power. How A. G. responded to my presentation in the meeting would determine whether the water packet program would go ahead as a nonprofit within P&G or would die a quiet death.

From prior meetings, I'd learned A. G. presents himself as almost professorial and is indeed very thoughtful. He'd brought P&G back to strong profitability after a recent downturn by helping the company get on the same page about our need to understand and serve consumers with our products. He started calling our consumer "her," understanding that it's mostly women who make purchase decisions about P&G products. And he coined the terms "first moment of truth" (when consumers are faced with a decision about which product to purchase) and "second moment of truth" (when consumers use our product). He helped P&G employees focus on winning at these two critical moments, and it was working.

Charlotte and I arrived at the boardroom before A. G. did. We positioned ourselves at the table so he would be sitting between us. I had brought some photos with me in case they'd be helpful to show A. G. the people we were trying to reach with our water purification packets. Sitting beside A. G. would allow me to easily show him the pictures.

I was keenly aware I was representing Mercy and Jemima and countless others like them in the boardroom of one of the most powerful corporations in the world. The stakes for them were incalculably great. I hoped I wouldn't let them down.

Soon A. G. walked in. His glasses and brushed-back white hair made him instantly recognizable. He greeted us and sat down.

We got straight to it. Charlotte began by giving A. G. the background on where the commercial water purification program was. "We set up test markets where we have distribution presence in Guatemala and the Philippines, and neither reached our expectations," she said. "We're currently testing the market in Pakistan, which has a great need for clean water. But again, the results are not encouraging."

A. G. was weighing Charlotte's words carefully.

Charlotte continued, "We recently had a meeting with the vice chair, and his response to creating a not-for-profit division within P&G was . . . let's say 'lukewarm.'"

"Why was that?" A. G. asked.

"Well," Charlotte said, "the vice chair noted that many of the people who tried the packets reported that they were a hassle to use. Five minutes of stirring, five minutes before pouring, and twenty *more* minutes of waiting—it takes a while." This was no surprise to me—I knew Charlotte would be truthful in reporting the vice chair's hesitancy. And it was true: In some places, especially where the water was not visibly dirty, people wondered whether the long cleaning process was worth the trouble. But Charlotte went further. "The vice chair thinks it's a turkey of a product."

This stunned me. Was she throwing me under the bus? I knew she had some hesitancy about setting up a not-for-profit business within her function, but I thought she'd come to terms with moving forward.

She glanced at me. All at once, I understood what she was doing. She wasn't pulling any punches—if this was going to move forward, she wanted to make sure she had given voice to the opposition. She was trying to define the two options distinctly in order to force a decisive response, one way or the other, from A. G.

My mind was racing. I decided I needed to show A. G. the picture of Mercy and her family collecting water out of the muddy pond. Meeting Mercy had shown me I was being called to help the world's poor in their life-or-death struggle for clean water, and maybe Mercy would have a similar effect on our CEO. I found the picture and held it tightly.

When I believed Charlotte was finished talking, I started moving my hand to show the picture to A. G.

Then Charlotte added, "So, A. G., you either believe Greg or the vice chair."

With Charlotte's unexpected ending, my hand jerked, and the picture went sailing through the air and landed in A. G.'s lap.

Now was the moment of truth. My first instinct was to apologize and carefully pick up the picture from his lap. But my second thought was that I was already in so deep that I might as well pretend throwing the picture was a sign of my confidence, an act of bravado.

I had A. G.'s attention. I said, "A. G., I'm going to address this on both an emotional and a rational level. First, look at that picture. For those people, it's not a hassle to use the packets to make their water clean. That pond is their only water source, and they share it with cattle." I didn't say it, but I could imagine him thinking about their "first moment of truth" in having an option provided by P&G to make their water clean versus a choice of contaminated water.

Then I explained our plans to create a not-for-profit business to provide the packets for emergency relief and social marketing. "With your approval, I'd like to enter two countries with the social-marketing approach—Haiti and Uganda. We need to see if people will really like using the products under direct circumstances." The "second moment of truth."

"So you want to enter two countries this year?" he asked. "How many countries are like these two?"

"UNICEF has a list of forty countries with high rates of death caused by unclean water," I replied. "That would be a place to start."

He asked a few more questions about the difference between the people in the test markets and Mercy's village. "It would be difficult for our distribution to reach Mercy's village in a cost-effective way," he acknowledged.

A. G. had listened intently, and now he was thinking through what we'd told him. He fidgeted with his glasses while Charlotte's stark alternative was hanging in the air: Would he believe me or believe the vice chair? As I waited for A. G.'s response, I felt like I was suffocating.

"I believe Greg," he said.

I felt like I could breathe again. The water packet *wasn't* a turkey of a product. It was worth risking a new approach for!

"The vice chair may be right," A. G. continued, "and we *might* fail with the packets. But Greg, if you don't give this project 110 percent of your effort, then we're *sure* to fail." A. G. looked like he was doing some calculation. "With forty countries, at two countries a year, we're looking at a twenty-year rollout. Greg, I want you to think of the twenty-year plan."

We thanked A. G. and he left. Charlotte congratulated me. "Okay, Greg," she said. "Get to work."

The nonprofit water program was a go.

7

HURRICANE IN HAITI

At this point, I knew A. G. and Charlotte's approval had a short leash. We were in no-man's-land with a current approval to move forward but no long-term plan for continued funding. I had created a house of cards that could fall apart with any wrong move.

Meanwhile, the water purification project got moved from the personal health care division to the sustainability division, so I was working under my supporter from Geneva, George Carpenter. I would be a department of one. No longer would I have to work on other products alongside the water project, so that reduced distractions. On the other hand, apart from some secretarial support and an eventual staff member, I would be doing this all on my own with only occasional help from other people. Everything, I felt, was on me.

As I'd told A. G., I wanted to start with safe drinking water pilot programs in Uganda and Haiti. Unlike in the earlier test marketing, now I wasn't looking for locations where we might have commercial success. Instead, I was identifying nations with a dramatic need for safer water. Both Haiti and Uganda had perpetual sickness from children drinking unsafe water.

I had seen the suffering in Haiti up close, and it fueled my passion to expand the Procter & Gamble program to have a bigger impact.

In the fall of 2004, before my meeting with A. G., I had been investigating the feasibility of social marketing for the packets in Haiti. It was during that time that Hurricane Jeanne bore down on Haiti. The storm killed more than three thousand people and devastated the town of Gonaïves. There was a great need for clean water, so we decided to put our investigations on hold and respond to the current emergency.

A couple of weeks after the hurricane hit, I flew to Haiti, accompanied by a US pastor who wanted to see the hurricane damage for himself.

The drive to Gonaïves took a long time because of washed-out roads. By the time the pastor and I arrived there, it was dark, and all the hotels on our list were full. The town was packed with personnel responding to the needs of the survivors or starting the rebuilding process. The only hotel we could find looked sketchy. We were told it had previously been a brothel.

I was given a large room with a big, round bed. This room had clearly once been opulent, but as with much of Gonaïves, the years had not been kind to it. The mattress had dark stains and a spring poking up through the middle. The large bathroom was missing many of its ceramic tiles. There was a massive tub in the middle of the bathroom, and a shower head extended from the ceiling to the center of the tub, but the shower handle had broken, and now it was jury-rigged with a rusty coat hanger.

I tried to sleep on the mattress, but the spring poking into my back made it impossible. I was reluctant to lie on the floor because of the bugs I'd seen scurrying back and forth, but after further attempts at sleep on the bed, I moved to the floor anyway. Despite my exhaustion, I got almost no rest that night. I wistfully thought of my family back home in Cincinnati and the relative luxury of our sleeping arrangements.

When the sun crept in through the curtains, I decided to forget about sleep and get ready for the important day ahead.

I brushed my teeth and shaved at a sink that was surprisingly small for such a massive bathroom. Then I stepped over the two-foot wall of the circular tub and pulled on the coat hanger to start the shower. As I got wet, I realized I'd forgotten to grab the soap off the sink. I jumped over the wall of the tub.

When I hit the tile, my wet feet flew out from under me, and I fell on my back, which knocked the breath out of me. My feet, now sticking straight up into the air, collided with the little ceramic sink, detaching it from the wall and sending it skyrocketing.

Still struggling to regain breath, I saw the sink heading right for my head. I caught it just in time. Water from the now-disconnected sink plumbing erupted into the air and rained down on me.

I laughed and shouted, "Good morning, Haiti!"

I thought the condition of the hotel might prepare me for what I saw in the country. But as run-down as the hotel was, it was nothing compared to what the people were enduring.

Everywhere I looked, there was destruction. And it affected the poorest people the most.

I met with some of Haiti's people and showed them how to use the purification packets. I went into a community where the water source was a large hand-dug open well fed by a spring. The floods from the hurricane had brought in debris, completely covering the surface of the water. I walked to the edge of the well to collect water in a bucket. I learned that in many emergencies we needed to provide buckets and cloths for filtering, since these items may have been washed away in the storm.

As I leaned to fill up the bucket, the water moved suddenly. I jumped back. I had disturbed a pig that was wallowing under the debris. I shouted my surprise, and the men and women who had gathered for the demonstration laughed. The pig was large, and a woman who spoke English told me, “She got in the water during the hurricane and hasn’t left. We think she was just as scared as us and feels safe here.” Then she added with a grin, “We’d appreciate if you can get her out. She’s using the water like a bathroom.”

I smiled back. “I don’t think I can help remove your pig,” I told her, “but I can show you how to purify your water.” I finished collecting the muddy water, added the packet, and stirred. When the magic moment of the water turning clear happened, the same woman said, “Man-o-man!” before switching to creole: “Dlo kristal!” (“crystal clear water”).

This community was similar to many others I visited who readily embraced the packets. Even though the stirring and filtering took time and effort, they were a small price to pay when people feared drinking from a water source contaminated by a disaster or following an outbreak of cholera. I saw that sustained use of the packets might be an issue with these same people, but when there was already a big disruption in their water access, they were willing to make the effort.

After several days of giving tutorials and distributing packets, the pastor and I traveled to Port-au-Prince, where we would stay overnight at the Hotel Montana before flying home. Many relief workers stayed at this hotel, which was a little island of French paradise separated from the chaos and poverty of the surrounding area. The contrast was stark and unsettling.

The pastor and I sat outside for dinner at a table overlooking the city below. We saw the glow from cook fires. The day’s heat died down, and the bustle of the day seemed to calm. We were debriefing about our time in Haiti.

"What has impressed me most," the pastor told me, "is the hospitality and warmth of the people. Even though they are living in extreme poverty and amid rampant corruption, they are still so generous with us."

I agreed. Earlier on this trip, one family offered to feed us lunch. They didn't have anything, so the husband set off to get some food. He couldn't find any. After more than an hour, we had to leave, but we were moved by the lengths this family was willing to go to in order to ensure we felt welcome.

We also recalled some of the more difficult experiences we had witnessed. "I can't get out of my head the woman whose child had dysentery," he told me. "To have to choose between the potential death of your child from dehydration or from bacteria-filled water that is likely fueling the dysentery . . ." He paused to find words to match the tragedy of the situation, especially as he realized that the woman's story was by no means unique. "It's heartbreaking."

"The poverty here is astonishing," I said. "More than once I've forgotten where I was and literally thought I was in rural Africa." The pastor nodded. "But what angers me is that I'm not twenty-four hours away in rural Africa. I'm a two-hour flight from Miami, one of the wealthiest places on the planet."

We sat there for a bit, both thinking, *Why is it this way, and what are we supposed to do about it?*

As we were having our heartfelt conversation, I heard some loud bangs from close by. Forgetting where I was, I commented to the pastor, "People must be shooting off fireworks." That's what it might have been if I'd heard those noises at home.

But this was not Cincinnati. This was Haiti.

A member of the International Rescue Committee, who had been sitting behind us, rushed over, grabbed us by our shirt collars, and yanked us to the ground. "Take cover!" he yelled. "Machine-gun fire!"

We froze under our table. We heard shouts and a few more bursts of gunfire. Then it was quiet for a few minutes before we heard the wailing of the people who had previously been serving us dinner.

When we were sure the gunfire had died down, we emerged from under the table.

We looked around. "What happened?"

"The owner of the hotel was just kidnapped," our waitress told us, sobbing.

We couldn't believe it.

"Was anyone injured?" I asked.

"No," she replied. "Thankfully, no one was shot."

Much later, we learned the owner of the hotel was returned unharmed after the hotel had paid a ransom.

This experience shook me. My heart broke for the people who had to live amid such chaos. I also reflected on my position. For a while I had known I was risking my career to bring water purification to people without making a profit, but until now I hadn't understood it also meant risking my life.

And it was risking my comfort as well. My time in Haiti brought into stark relief the conditions of the people I was trying to help. I lived a largely comfortable life with my family in Cincinnati. Why did I have clean, running water in the kitchen as well as many bathrooms throughout the house while so many in Haiti were surrounded by violence and devastation? Why was I living in comparative luxury when hundreds of millions of people had to walk to contaminated water sources, at the mercy of parasites and diseases?

When I returned from my travels, I would lie awake in my bed, thinking about this disparity.

Throughout the rest of 2004, I spent most of my time traveling between Uganda and Haiti, working to ensure successful launches of our social-marketing effort. I was in Uganda having dinner one evening early in December when Keith Zook called me. Keith was a member of the corporate sustainability group who had some extra capacity, so he supported my work and eventually joined my team. I'd asked him to lead the communications with our manufacturing plant in Pakistan to ensure we had enough supply of the water packets and later to manage the shipping of the packets around the world. Keith told me the plant manager had called to tell him they needed to shut down production. It turned out the commercial effort in Pakistan had been even less successful than was being communicated to us. To gain distribution, our team had promised our customers—the distributors supplying the packets to shops—that we would accept return of any product not sold. The plant manager had explained to Keith that they were receiving load after load of returned product to the plant.

"How should we respond?" Keith asked me.

"Give me a day to think about it," I said.

At this point, we'd sold three million packets in three years of test markets. Now the plant in Pakistan was filling up with product that would likely expire before we could use it. I had no idea how successful selling the product at cost for emergency relief or our social marketing efforts would be. But I had also just recently seen how effective they were during the emergency in Haiti. I had a sleepless night pondering the next move and prayed for guidance.

In the morning, I called Keith. "Well, Keith, the company has given me responsibility for this program," I explained. "I don't know what will happen with our social-marketing efforts, but we're fully committed to them. Maybe they'll take off."

Keith was silent.

I continued, "What I'm really worried about if we shut down manufacturing is that there will be a big global disaster where the product is needed, and we'll not have enough to respond."

I paused. "Tell the plant to keep running."

Big global disaster? I didn't know where those words came from. Even at the time it seemed to me, and probably to Keith, like a leap in logic. We had a product *surplus*, which I was worried about expiring, and I was telling the factory to produce *more*?

Yet that decision changed everything.

The plant kept running, and we built up a stockpile of thirteen million packets. The plant had to rent space to store all of them.

I headed home for what I thought would be a restful and uninterrupted Christmas vacation, little knowing the consequences my decision would have.

8

PLUNGED INTO PROMINENCE

By December 2004 I was exhausted. I was also feeling guilty about missing so much time with my family over the last quarter of the year as I was trying to get Procter & Gamble's packet business off the ground. I believed the job was worth the long hours and the wear and tear on my body. *Everything* was on the line to make the not-for-profit effort a success and to help people in desperate situations. But I also knew it was taking a toll on my wife and kids to have me gone so much.

In fact, right before the hurricane in Haiti, when my job was under threat, we had moved because of the difficulty my absence was creating for the rest of the family. Our old house was across town from our daughter Meredith's school, dance, and gymnastics, and with me traveling so frequently, my wife was responsible for almost all the shuttling required to get her where she needed to be. I knew she was carrying a heavy burden largely by herself. And I could tell my daughters also felt my absence.

At a rare dinner I was able to eat at home, I told my family, "I know I've been gone a lot in the past few months." I received looks like that was a charitable way to put it. I ventured, "I know this has been hard on you, but I'm going to make it up to you. The holidays are coming up, and I promise I will take a break from work."

"No BlackBerry?" my daughter Meredith asked.

I hesitated. I didn't know if I could truly go without my mobile phone. But I eventually caved. "No BlackBerry."

Despite my family's doubtful glances, I believed what I said.

We drove to New Jersey to be with my wife's family. The visit started well, with wonderful celebrations on Christmas Day.

The day after Christmas, we took a long walk along the Palisades, a scenic line of cliffs on the lower Hudson River. I congratulated myself for turning off my BlackBerry and leaving it in the car. On the walk I took a deep breath of relaxation and reacquainted myself with the day-to-day concerns of my wife and daughters. It felt good to be fully present with them after so long away.

When I returned to the car, I turned on my BlackBerry, just in case someone needed to reach me in an emergency. I looked at the notifications, and I saw that the news was filled with reports of a tremendous tsunami ravaging coastline communities around the Indian Ocean.

The earthquake, which occurred off the coast of Sumatra, Indonesia, was one of the largest ever recorded. It created a tsunami that struck the coasts of at least fourteen nations, swiftly killing more than two hundred thousand people. The wall of seawater either disabled or contaminated nearly all the drinking water sources near the areas where the tsunami hit. Everyone from emergency relief experts to pundits in the media focused on the expected second wave of deaths from diarrheal illness caused by unsafe water.

In no time, the hundred-foot-high waves that hit Banda Aceh washed away my commitment to spend time with my family. This disaster was going to draw me in, as if in the backwash of the mighty wave. My phone started ringing almost immediately, and it didn't stop. Because of the time difference, it kept ringing day and night.

P&G convened a crisis team led by our Asia Pacific senior leader Bob McDonald. (Bob would later go on to become P&G's CEO and then the US Secretary of Veteran Affairs.) We started each of our early calls with an update on efforts to find our Thailand country manager. She had been vacationing by the sea in Thailand over the Christmas holiday, and we knew she had run from the tsunami, but she had not been located. When we eventually learned she did not survive, the tragedy became deeply personal for our team.

Bob helped us understand that water was the key issue in this emergency and we should respond with the packets. I strongly agreed and urged the company to continue with our plan to sell the packets at cost while also offering grants through our philanthropic arm, the P&G Fund, to help with the distribution and training needed for the packets. Even now, I wanted to make sure we would be able to provide packets in the future as well, not just for this immediate emergency.

Within a week, we sold all the packets we had in storage, and the Pakistani plant's space was freed up so they could crank out as many of the packets as possible. Given where we'd come from, this was a miracle. We had sold three million packets in three years of unsuccessful test markets. Now, within a short time, we had sold *thirteen* million packets. If I hadn't told the plant just weeks earlier to keep running, we would never have been able to have this impact.

I spent hour after hour talking to representatives from relief organizations so they'd understand we had packets available and also offering P&G's philanthropic funds. There were huge logistical challenges in getting the packets out of Pakistan, and resolving these also took many hours on the phone.

All this, by the way, was happening while I was still in New Jersey, supposedly spending a relaxing Christmas with my family.

In retrospect, it would have been better if I had just apologized to my family for having to work after all and then left to focus on the emergency. Instead, I tried to pretend I was still spending quality time with them while simultaneously dealing with an international emergency. While we were visiting the sights—the New York Botanical Garden, the Metropolitan Museum of Art, and Central Park—I was constantly on the phone making arrangements. And worse, I'm very loud when I'm on the phone. So not only was I not fully present with them, but I also ruined my family's ability to enjoy themselves. Not surprisingly, they were sullen and losing patience with me.

I felt horrible about breaking my promise to spend time with them. But instead of apologizing, I tried to justify my efforts. At dinner with my family and my in-laws, I estimated how many lives we could potentially impact because of what I was doing. I don't remember the specifics of my calculation (and given my exhaustion, the calculations were likely inaccurate), but I truly believed that my personal actions over the course of this holiday would impact thousands of lives. "Thank you for sacrificing your holiday," I told them. "Your sacrifice is helping many people in trouble."

While what I said was true, a simple apology from me would have gone a long way toward reducing the tension. The responsibility of responding to the massive crisis felt like a heavy weight, which, when combined with my guilt over disappointing my family, resulted in my crying myself to sleep several of the nights we were there. We ended up cutting our holiday short and drove home to Cincinnati early. I made preparations to fly to Pakistan and then to Sri Lanka to help with the relief efforts while my family finished their holiday break at home without me.

I was working around the clock once I hit the ground in Pakistan at the beginning of the new year. Because of the time differences, during the day I worked with the Pakistan team to get the product out of the country, and then at night I worked with US-based NGOs and P&G people in Cincinnati. By the time I made it to Sri Lanka, I was more exhausted than I'd ever been.

I had dinner with some of our NGO partners at my hotel in Colombo, Sri Lanka. The following night I saw some people I recognized from an NGO and went to introduce myself. "Hi, it's good to see you guys here," I said. "I've been here helping with education on the P&G packets."

They looked at one another quizzically. "Yes, we know, Greg," one of them said. "We met you at dinner last night."

My face grew hot, and I faked an excuse. I realized I was so tired, I was having amnesia. Only vaguely could I remember dinner the prior evening.

My health and well-being were beginning to suffer, but just as I had with my family, I rationalized it was worth it to make sure this program succeeded. It wasn't just that I knew the effort had a short leash following A. G.'s agreement to try the not-for-profit approach. But more immediately, we had an opportunity to provide urgently needed, life-changing help for some of the survivors of the tsunami. Looking back, I can see that I probably had an unhealthy desire to be a hero. Yet I wouldn't let up.

Up to this point I had been focusing on educating the many NGO partners who had purchased the product. I had not yet visited the areas of Sri Lanka where we were providing the packets. I knew I needed to see the effort firsthand and report back to P&G, so I hired a taxi driver to help me reach some parts of the island where the devastation had been the worst and where, hopefully, I could see the packets being put to good use.

Many of the roads were damaged by the tsunami and were jammed with relief vehicles bringing aid. I woke at four a.m. to join the line of vehicles slowly making their way down the coast. I was able to visit several locations and provide counsel on proper use of the packets.

This was one of hundreds of disaster areas I would visit over the years. I learned a few things with this one. First, during a disaster, clean water was often a recognized need, and response groups were eager to have a tool that could be easily deployed. Second, the water sources that disaster victims had access to were frequently not their usual ones, so it was easy to have them use the P&G packets while waiting for their normal water source to be restored. Third, P&G employees were grateful we were responding—so grateful that eventually an expectation developed that we would respond and that I would post updates from the disaster areas.

One of our most emotional stops in Sri Lanka was to see the remains of a train that had been struck by the tsunami. The train had been tossed about like it was a toy. Its cars were filled with mud and vegetation that had been swept into them by the waves. There were no longer any bodies in them, but we could see blood among the broken glass.

Visiting Hikkaduwa, we learned that more than sixteen hundred people there had perished in the rushing water. The waves traveled more than two miles inland at this location. Because people's homes were destroyed, in excess of two hundred thousand people were now clustered in camps. I met the village mayor and arranged for more packets to be delivered from one of our partners.

In Galle I visited a refugee camp and met Mohamed Irshad, a man in his thirties living in a blue tent with his family. He was shirtless and wore a sarong. He and his family seemed to be in shock. The waves had reached five feet high in his home almost a mile from the ocean. The home was still standing, but they couldn't move back in because it was filled with mud. They spent their nights in the camp and their days cleaning up the mess. Their only option for drinking water was well water that looked thoroughly disgusting because the waves had brought debris into the well.

The P&G packets had no problem purifying the well water, and soon we were drinking clean water together. I was able to provide the Irshad family with enough packets to clean their water for a month while their well was rehabilitated.

During our drive along the Sri Lankan coast, I trained Dava, my taxi driver, in how to use the video camera I'd purchased for the trip so I could record my experiences to share with P&G employees. He filmed me speaking outside Le Grand Hotel, which had survived the flood because it was located on a hill.

I visited different areas, teaching people how to use the packets, until the sun was starting to go down. Sitting in the back seat of the taxi, I could finally relax a bit and decided to nap. As soon as I dozed off, though, I was jolted awake remembering I had not yet returned a call from *The Wall Street Journal*. They had called me days earlier, wanting to write a story on P&G's tsunami response. I felt a sudden urge to act.

In my exhaustion I forgot about the time difference and called the reporter, Sarah Ellison, in New York City from my mobile.

She answered sleepily, but when she realized what the call was about, she quickly got to the point. "The *Journal* is interested in running a story on P&G's water efforts," she said, "but we need a hook of a specific story. Ideally it would include a picture of a beneficiary using the P&G packets."

I told her, "I visited areas today that might be great for your story, but I'm currently returning to Colombo and will fly back to the US early tomorrow. What a shame I didn't know earlier! I could have connected with one of your local journalists."

"Where are you right now?" Sarah asked.

I looked outside and could still see Le Grand Hotel, high on its hill. "I'm in Galle," I replied.

"Galle, Galle . . ." I heard her checking her notes. "We have a reporter staying at Le Grand Hotel!" she said excitedly. "Eric Bellman." Sarah gave me his number.

I called Eric, and within minutes we were headed to the home of Mohamed Irshad, whom I'd visited earlier that day. Less than an hour later, just as the sun was setting, the journalist had his story.

The Wall Street Journal ran Sarah and Eric's story titled "Clean Water, No Profit" on the cover of the *Journal*'s Marketplace section.[1] Bob McDonald congratulated me and said the story was a boon for P&G's reputation and consistent with our purpose to improve lives. In fact, many of the people within P&G who had opposed or been lukewarm to the idea of the nonprofit water purifier distribution now expressed their support. Our tsunami response not only helped a lot of people, but it also broadened the view of many at P&G on the potential for the not-for-profit effort.

P&G's work was now being mentioned in many news stories about how people and organizations were responding to the tsunami. We were aided by the fact that Senator Bill Frist—at the time the Republican majority leader of the Senate—had visited Indonesia and spoken to the media about how the P&G packets were useful in helping survivors. Senator Frist was one of the first of many high-profile politicians I would work with on both sides of the aisle. I didn't care much about politics. I was eager to work with anyone who could help shine a spotlight on the global water crisis and P&G's role in addressing it.

I was asked to present P&G's efforts at the United Nations

Headquarters in New York at an event hosted by former Presidents George H. W. Bush and Bill Clinton and by Hank McKinnell, head of Business Roundtable and the CEO of Pfizer. Following my presentation, McKinnell was effusive in his praise for P&G's efforts. This was quite a surprise to me, as I knew Pfizer was one of the most significant contributors to the tsunami response. When this type of recognition occurred again and again, it became apparent that the P&G effort was receiving so much attention because it was simple to understand and meeting a clear need.

Our tsunami response was a boost for our emergency relief efforts by allowing many organizations to gain firsthand experience with the packets, and this resulted in repeat sales. I continued to believe our social marketing efforts could also be a valuable way to help more people beyond emergency situations.

P&G received awards for our work with victims of the tsunami. One of them was the Stockholm Industry Water Award. This meant a trip to Sweden to meet with King Carl XVI Gustaf.

My private conversation with the king was my first experience with royalty, so I wasn't sure of the protocol or what to talk about. On the way to Sweden, I'd visited the slums of Mumbai, India, where the packets were helping survivors of flooding. I mentioned this work to King Gustaf, and it didn't seem to resonate with him. Panicking, I realized the conversation was falling flat. But eventually we found common ground discussing changing weather patterns associated with climate change. He was a strong environmental advocate. The rest of the conversation went well.

The celebratory dinner after the award ceremony was held in the Nobel Hall, where Nobel laureates are honored, and I felt privileged to represent P&G in such a place.

Even though I'd written a vision statement that mentioned the praise of kings, I never expected this would literally come true. Now I was reminded of God's message to me in Geneva—*Do you doubt I can do this?*—and felt he was enabling me to accomplish the audacious vision I had written down.

9

TWO CENTS' WORTH

In April 2007 I flew to Washington, DC, to receive the Strategic Vision Award from the Center for Strategic and International Studies. I must admit to taking a bit of selfish pleasure in this particular award, because when I'd been promoting the not-for-profit effort within Procter & Gamble, one of my critics had accused me of lacking "strategic vision." And here I was, receiving an award for exactly that quality and for the exact same business! I felt like I'd come a long way.

That same day I had been in New York for what would turn out to be a meeting of more long-lasting significance. This was my first time attending the Clinton Global Initiative (CGI) annual meeting.

The CGI annual meeting brings together global leaders to address the world's most pressing problems. P&G became an active participant in CGI because the meeting was effective in building awareness of our clean drinking water efforts. Former President Bill

Clinton himself would frequently highlight P&G's clean drinking water efforts, including on the *Today* show and *David Letterman*. So in addition to the praise of kings, our program was receiving the praise of presidents. Because of participating in CGI, P&G would eventually develop partnerships with World Vision, Africare, the Jane Goodall Institute, FXB International, Students of the World, and FHI 360.

The CGI annual meeting is unlike other meetings because it puts a spotlight on good works through a formal process of making concrete, tangible commitments. CGI staff work with commitment makers to craft an agreement, which is then reported on and evaluated using chosen metrics. It's a rigorous and deliberate process to ensure that progress is made toward addressing the world's problems.

At this first CGI meeting, I participated in a conversation between former President Bill Clinton and Jim Stengel, P&G's chief marketing officer at the time. Clinton urged us, among other things, to get together with Roy Spence, the cofounder of GSD&M advertising agency in Austin, Texas. Clinton had worked with Roy since Clinton's days as governor of Arkansas. The president believed Roy might be able to help us spread the word about our purification packets.

When Jim and I met with Roy Spence in Austin a few weeks later, I showed Roy the magic of the P&G packets. He became excited and peppered me with questions.

Roy asked, "How much does one packet treat?"

"Ten liters," I answered.

"How much does it cost to provide one of those packets?"

"Ten cents."

"One penny per liter?"

"Yes, sir," I answered.

Roy asked, "How much water does a person usually drink in a day?"

"Two liters," I responded.

Roy thought for a few seconds and then said, "Two pennies a day?"

"Yes, sir."

With his strong Texas accent, Roy said, "Well, sir, I'd give my two cents' worth to save a life."

Roy and Jim went on talking while I only half listened. I'd become fixated on what Roy had just said. Prior to this, I'd often told people that we could provide water at one penny per liter, but Roy's colloquialism made the same point more effectively and more memorably.

I still can't quite believe what I did next. I jotted on a piece of paper "I, Roy Spence, give freely for all time without prejudice and with no compensation the phrase 'give your two cents to save a life' to Greg Allgood for use at his discretion forever, for any purpose he chooses." Then I left space for Roy to sign.

Interrupting the conversation, I said, "Roy, you're the marketer, and I'm the scientist, but I really, really love 'Give your two cents to save a life.' May I please have it?"

He looked at me with his head cocked. Then he grinned. "Sure!" He signed my hand-scrawled—and hardly legal—contract.

The day after I returned from Austin, Keith Zook told me about an American Express contest in which Amex card members could enter their idea to save the world. The winner of the contest would be awarded one million dollars for their cause. In the first round of voting, Amex card members could vote for their favorite entries to give them some ranking. A panel of celebrity judges would then pick their top fifty entries, which would go on to compete based solely on the second round of card member votes. The top vote getter in this runoff of fifty entries would receive the one-million-dollar prize.

When I'd asked Roy Spence for ownership of the phrase "Give your two cents to save a life," I only knew I liked it. I had no idea how I would use it. Now, within twenty-four hours, I'd been given a wonderful opportunity. I filled out the online forms for the Amex contest. My entry popped up among hundreds of others, which later grew to more than seven thousand, with each entry showing the total votes gained.

It didn't take long before my entry started to get a lot of votes. Within days, it was in the top ten. Pushing a good thing along, I sent emails to my friends and mentioned the contest in my blog to encourage P&G colleagues—almost all of whom had an Amex Corporate Card—to vote. My entry moved into the top five by the end of the first round of voting.

I looked at the list of celebrity judges to see if I could predict anything about what might appeal to them. To my delight, I saw that my hero Jane Goodall was among the judges. Luckily, there were no top vote getters promoting ideas to save the chimps!

In time, the final fifty entries were announced, and I'd made it through to the second round. It looked like the judges pretty much picked the top fifty based on the highest vote receivers in the first round. The vote count was set back to zero for all entries, with two weeks to determine the final winner.

I asked Susan Arnold, the vice chair of P&G, to send a note to all employees (about 125,000 at the time) encouraging people to vote. I thought we were cruising to victory.

Then disaster hit, or at least it nearly did.

Online chatter accused P&G of using its muscle to win the Amex contest. A lot of this was coming from one particular nonprofit that had its own entry in the final round. They were making the case that this situation was like David versus Goliath, with their nonprofit being the shepherd boy and P&G being the evil giant. They were out to slay us, and it seemed to be working—they were generating outrage and support for their position.

I hadn't seen this coming. What harm could there be in getting attention for a good cause in a fun contest? The fact is, I was naive in thinking there would be no downsides in something where a significant amount of money was at stake. Nevertheless, I thought the controversy would play out in the blogosphere and not have much effect on P&G or the contest.

Then *The New York Times* called.

The reporter was Claudia Deutsch. We had met several times during my years as the external relations leader for P&G's personal health care business. I had previously shared with her some of the journey of our safe drinking water efforts. Claudia told me, "My editor asked me to do a story about the American Express contest. I'm surprised there's been so much controversy."

This was not good. Unlike the earlier situation I'd managed with the National Park Service, negative controversy about our clean drinking water program could be a fatal blow to the effort. Given how closely the P&G Children's Safe Drinking Water Program was tied to the P&G corporate name, it was critical that the controversy not damage P&G broadly. Despite the risk, I was determined to leverage winning the contest to build the program and not let it hurt P&G's reputation.

Perhaps because of my zealous determination, I did something I shouldn't have done and that was not aligned with my P&G managers. "Can I go off the record?" I asked Claudia. I felt I needed to give her the backstory about the potential negative impact of the contest on our clean drinking water work. Going off the record is a risk, and any PR agency will tell you never to do this. But I felt I had no alternative.

"Sure," Claudia agreed.

I told her my dilemma. "This controversy means we probably should not take the risk of staying in the contest," I said, "because one million dollars is nothing compared to the countless lives we would change with the P&G water program if we continue the work."

Claudia knew I wasn't blowing smoke. She knew from our previous conversations that I had risked my career for the program.

After listening to me, Claudia asked, "Now can *I* go off the record?" The journalist asking the interviewee to go off the record—that was a first for me! But I agreed, of course.

Claudia took an aggressive tone and said, "Don't you dare pull your entry. You're the only one I've interviewed for this story who is focused on their cause versus the fairness of the contest." She further said that, while she wouldn't tell me the details, she felt confident P&G would think the story was balanced and it would reflect what she'd been told in her interviews.

"Okay," I told Claudia. "I'll stay in."

I had a restless night waiting for the story to run. The next day I saw Claudia's story, and it was indeed balanced. In fact, I was the only person quoted who was talking about the cause: "The whole reason I'm doing this is to save kids' lives . . . and I don't want to do anything that would interfere with that mission."[1]

The online version of the *New York Times* story included a link to vote in the contest. This was phenomenal free advertising for American Express, and readers responded. My entry pulled ahead and won the contest.

And then more controversy happened. But luckily this part was behind the scenes.

I had requested that the winnings go to a partner who would donate P&G packets to some of the neediest people around the world, but Amex explained they had the right to select whomever they wanted as the recipient of the funds, and they wanted UNICEF to receive the money. This frustrated me. UNICEF was a good partner—they used our product in emergencies—but I thought I should have the freedom to pick the partner and not Amex.

I had several calls with Amex personnel, trying and failing to get us all on the same page. Then Amex told me they had made a final decision: They would give the funds to UNICEF, but they would increase the prize amount to *two* million dollars and request that

UNICEF designate the funds for providing clean water, albeit not specify the P&G packets.

The more selfish part of me was still upset because I knew how effective our work with the packets could be with an additional million dollars. But the more objective part of me was pleased that now *two* million dollars would be donated to provide clean water in some manner to the people who needed it most. The more objective half of me spoke up. I thanked the Amex team for the additional million dollars. "This is going to help so many people."

They invited me to New York for a media tour to announce the winner. The biggest interview was a live appearance on CBS's *The Early Show*. I offered to memorize and personalize the messages Amex wanted to get across, delivering them when talking with the TV show hosts. The Amex people were shocked that a scientist like me was fluent in public relations. They were elated with how the interview had gone.

In return, I asked them for a favor. "Could you tell me if Jane Goodall looked at my entry?"

They checked their records and told me Jane Goodall had seen my entry—*and* selected it to go into the final round of the contest. Wow! Along with Jacques Cousteau, Jane Goodall had been one of my childhood heroes, one of the people responsible for putting me on my current path, and here I was just one step away from her.

But it gets better.

Jane Goodall was announced as one of the speakers for the next Clinton Global Initiative meeting. I was determined to take this occasion to meet her. The CGI personnel allowed me access to the green room where Jane was preparing to go on the main stage. I introduced myself, but before I could explain about winning the Amex contest, she said, "I know who you are." We had a pleasant, though brief, conversation. She asked me to meet with Bill Johnston, the president of the Jane Goodall Institute, to see if we could collaborate in using the packets to bring clean water to the villages surrounding where the chimps live on Gombe Island, Tanzania.

"If we're going to help the chimps," Jane said, "we also have to help the people living near them. I know there's a lot of sickness from bad water. And these people are my friends. I'd love it if you could help make their drinking water safer."

I met with Bill, and a few months later I found myself jumping off a cargo barge onto the shores of Gombe. I saw the places Jane had stood all those years ago viewing the chimps, and I saw quite a few chimps myself. I collaborated with her institute for several years in providing the packets, and I'm so grateful to have had the opportunity to connect with one of my heroes.

"Two cents to save a life" turned out to be a very good deal indeed. A lot of my work with P&G's water program involved dealing with money and strategy and with colleagues and partners. And although it could frequently be a lot of fun, it was impossible for me to forget what it was really all about: providing clean water to people in great need.

10

PLAYING THE HERO

When Procter & Gamble officially branded the P&G Children's Safe Drinking Water Program,[1] they didn't want it to come across as a faceless corporate effort and thus go unnoticed. So Charlotte Otto and Jim Stengel (P&G's chief marketing officer) suggested that a P&G person should be seen as the leader of the work. P&G decided to, in essence, brand *me* as "Dr. Allgood" to act as the face of the program. Reluctant as I was to become a mascot, I knew this would build credibility and visibility and thereby secure P&G support for the program. And with the previous PR work I had done for the company, this was a natural fit.

For a long time I'd had a standard way of introducing myself to people: "Hi, I'm Dr. Greg Allgood, but you can call me Water Boy." I wanted people to recognize my credentials but also to realize I was approachable. But with the branding effort, the Dr. Greg Allgood persona became most prominent.

Part of my role was to engage our employees, so I was asked to write a blog about the program. Initially published in January 2005, this eventually became P&G's first external blog. P&G employees around the world followed it closely, and the blog helped inspire them in their own work because P&G's efforts to provide clean water were possible only through the success of their work on P&G brands.

The program was clearly resonating with P&G employees. But even though I had agreed with the decision to brand "Dr. Greg Allgood" as the face of the program, I at times felt uncomfortable with this level of visibility.

My discomfort grew when the program started to win awards. There were many people supporting P&G's clean water effort, and I felt that putting one person in the spotlight could diminish the visibility of their work. At one point I started sending my teammate Keith Zook to receive the awards. Another reason the branding was unsettling was because I was working with people in the not-for-profit world who were getting paid less than I was and were receiving little attention for their efforts. *They* deserved awards more than *I* did.

As unsettling as this was, an experience with P&G employees helped put my branding in perspective.

One year for World Water Day (March 22), P&G blew up a picture of me near a mud pond in Africa and installed a green screen in the lobby of our headquarters so employees could get a picture with "Dr. Greg."

My secretary, Peg Fortenbery, told me, "There are hundreds of people waiting in line to get a picture with your life-size photo, Greg."

"Really?" I had a hard time believing so many people would show up to get a picture with *me*.

"I'm serious. I was just there and saw it for myself. Why don't you go down and talk with them?"

I decided I might as well.

I walked up to several different employees in line and introduced myself. Many of the conversations went about the same.

"Hi, I'm Dr. Greg Allgood with the Children's Safe Drinking Water Program. That's my picture up there you're in line for."

"Oh, is that right? Nice to meet you."

"Let me tell you a little about what I do."

They'd listen for a bit, but then their attention would wander. Maybe they'd look over my shoulder or smile at a friend. I could see they were losing interest. But even as they lost interest in *me*, they stayed in line for the picture.

This made me realize something: They weren't interested in meeting me. They wanted some personal association with the *brand.*

I was taken aback by this at first. Then the humor of the situation struck me. After all, the work wasn't about me, anyway. "Dr. Greg" was just a symbol of P&G's good work, and if that helped the cause, that was a good thing. In fact, it gradually became clearer to me that I could use this branding to shine a spotlight on the people we were helping and on our partners.

But this persona also made me, at times, feel like playing the hero, ready to ride in on a white horse and save those who needed my help. And it was sometimes hard to distinguish between the real me and "Dr. Greg Allgood" the brand.

When I was a teenager, I took lifeguard training because I loved being in and around the water and thought it would be a useful skill. Twice as a young man I had used that training to save people who might have drowned otherwise. I didn't really expect to call on my lifesaving skills again many years later.

In 2008 my family was on a spring break vacation to Cabo San Lucas, Mexico. One afternoon, when my family wanted to rest, I rented a kayak and paddled alone across the bay to the famous Arch. Once I passed the Arch, I was no longer in the Gulf of California and was now paddling in the Pacific Ocean. The waves were mild in the bay but were about four feet high on the Pacific Ocean side.

Not far past the Arch, I heard screams. I looked around and saw two women, probably in their twenties, standing on a bit of beach and waving and screaming.

"Help! Someone help us!"

The young women's abandoned Jet Ski was tumbling from side to side near the shore. Waves were breaking on the tiny beach, and the incoming tide would soon engulf their last bit of dry land.

I quickly assessed the situation. Several motorboats had gathered near the scene, but they were likely keeping their distance because if they got too close to the beach, they would become stranded just like the young women, such were the size and power of the waves. I wasn't sure if they'd radioed for help or tried to communicate with the young women. All I knew was these women needed help—fast.

Without thinking, I paddled over to one of the motorboats. "Would you hold my kayak?" I asked the people onboard. "I'm going to help those young women." When they agreed, I rolled off and swam toward the beach.

I developed a plan while I swam. I didn't think the situation was dangerous as long as I could calm them down. A panicking person will often do whatever they can to get out of the water, including grabbing at their rescuer and forcing them under. It's not unusual for someone trying to save a drowning person to be drowned in the process. So I knew I needed to prevent the women from panicking, as that would make it harder to bring them to safety. I had been reading one of Clive Cussler's novels about adventurer and scuba diver Dirk Pitt. I decided to pretend to be a hero like Dirk, thinking that might put them at ease.

The swim to the beach took longer than expected because I was swimming against a strong current. With the big waves, I went under a few times. But I dug into my strokes and kicked harder. I made it to the beach gassed.

Once I was nearly out of the water, the two women rushed toward me. Trying not to reveal how winded I was (because Dirk Pitt wouldn't show weakness), I asked, "What happened?"

"We got too close to the shore with our Jet Ski," one of them said, almost hysterically. "A big wave pushed us near the beach, and then another knocked us off!"

"And when that happened," the other woman said, "the keys to the Jet Ski fell out, and they must have washed away."

"Now we're stuck!" the first woman added.

I looked them in the eye. "Listen," I said. "You're going to be okay. I'm a certified lifeguard and scuba diver. I've done this before. No one is going to get hurt today. I'm going to save you."

My Dirk Pitt routine worked. The young women no longer seemed scared.

"Which of you is the stronger swimmer?" I asked. They both acknowledged the second woman. I told her, "Stay here. I'll come back for you in a minute. I'm going to take her first." I took the first woman by the hand to help her through the waves and pulled her into a lifeguard hold. I sidestroked with her to one of the motorboats. Then I went back for the second woman.

Just as I helped the second woman onto the motorboat, the Mexican Navy arrived with their sirens sounding and lights blazing. The motorboats must have radioed them before I swam to shore. They collected us all on their vessel. We explained what had happened.

The young women were thankful. "Who are you?" they asked.

I kept up the Dirk Pitt routine. In a deeper voice than normal, I said, "My name is Dr. Allgood. I travel around the world helping save people's lives with clean water."

They fell for my hero act and cheered at their good fortune. "Really, your name is Allgood?" they said. "Thank you for saving us!"

The Navy officer said, "We can take you and your kayak back across the bay."

But still in hero mode, I said, "I paddled out here, and I'll paddle back." I made my exit with a running headfirst dive off the boat and took the few strokes back to my kayak.

When I told this story to my teenage daughters, Ashton and Meredith, they rolled their eyes at my heroic Dr. Allgood act. All along I hadn't thought there was much danger involved, so I'd been approaching it lightheartedly. But when I thought about it more deeply, there *was* a way in which at this time in my career I had a superhero complex. I believed that, without my sacrifices, the water program would stand no chance at P&G and that, without my efforts, countless thousands of people might die. The understanding that the global water crisis was life-or-death seemed clearer to me than it did to others around me, and I took it very seriously. Early in the clean water effort, I'd had to go it alone, and I still harbored that lone-wolf impulse.

Later that same year, my family and I took a trip to Fiji. We hadn't gotten enough of water after our time in Mexico, and now we yearned to scuba dive in the tropical waters of the South Pacific and see some of the most beautiful underwater scenes in the world. We weren't disappointed in our dives in the ripping currents off Taveuni, Fiji. The soft corals have a kaleidoscope of colors and extend themselves to feed in the currents, appearing almost to bloom. We swam with whitetip sharks and manta rays.

Following one of our dives, we had the opportunity to hike to a nearby waterfall. My family was reluctant because we had another dive scheduled later in the day and they wanted to rest. I'm usually restless, even on vacation. In fact, Ashton has said that I lead great trips, but they are never vacations because they are so packed with activities.

In the end, I talked them into it with a line borrowed from Jimmy Buffett. "You can't sit around and wait for adventure," I said. "Besides, it will be fun."

Meredith answered, "Yes, blue-eyed prince." She came up with that nickname to tease me for playing the hero, and it stuck. (She has since shortened it to BEP.)

My family was joined on the hike by four other travelers and a local guide. We bumped along a dirt road in a jeep to reach a trailhead in the rainforest. From there, we hiked through the thick undergrowth, crisscrossing a stream several times.

On one section of our trail, the path was slippery from recent rain, and there was a sheer drop on one side to the stream about thirty feet below. My family was a bit ahead of me. I noticed the danger and was just about to warn my girls to be careful when I saw two people fall down the precipice. Our guide had fallen with one of the people hiking with us—a young woman I knew slightly, named Brandy. I heard a sharp *crack*! With horror, I realized that was the sound of Brandy's head hitting rock.

Without thinking, I scrambled down the cliff to help. Brandy lay on a little rock island in the stream, bleeding from the lower back of her head. Her pupils were dilated. She seemed unconscious. I was worried she might die in front of me.

Unlike my time playing the hero in Mexico, I knew Dr. Allgood couldn't save Brandy alone. I silently prayed for God to use me to help her.

Then the strangest thing happened. I felt God's power running through me. Clarity and purpose focused me. I sensed God telling me I could help Brandy and needed to bring her back.

Leaning close to the young woman's ear, I kept repeating, "Brandy, come back. Brandy, come back to me."

She began to respond. She was not speaking, but I could see consciousness return to her eyes.

The guide, who had sustained only minor injuries from his fall, brushed himself off and went for help. Even though we couldn't see each other, my family and I were able to communicate, and we made sure everyone was all right. They and the other hikers returned to the hotel when the guide went to get help. They weren't surprised when I said I was going to stay and help Brandy.

I repositioned myself where I could prevent her from falling off the rock if she began to move. Just as I was remembering that one sign of traumatic head injury is vomiting, Brandy retched, throwing up violently. After that, she responded more and more to me. She could return the squeeze to my hand and follow the movement of my finger with her eyes, and she was starting to speak.

Our conversation was repetitive.

"I'm confused. Where am I?" she'd say. "What happened?" She didn't remember her name or what country she was in.

I'd tell her everything I knew about her from prior conversations we'd had on a dive boat and explain what had happened.

She would smile slightly, look into my eyes, and say, "Thank you." Then it would start again. "I'm confused. Where am I? What happened?"

Two and a half hours after the injury, a team of local men arrived with a stretcher. We slowly moved Brandy off the ledge and carried her down the stream. We found a place to reenter the trail and then drove her into town, with me bracing her against the jolts from the bumpy road.

At the clinic, Brandy was comforted by my now-familiar face, so I stayed with her while the medical personnel put an IV into her arm to bring up her fluid level. X-rays revealed no injuries besides a hairline fracture in the back of her skull. A trauma surgeon arrived at about two in the morning and took over, so I headed back to the hotel. There were some medical mission personnel staying at the hotel, as well as several other vacationers. I let them know how Brandy was doing, and we signed up in one-hour shifts to stay with Brandy and make sure she was okay.

On the afternoon of the following day, those of us who had been caring for Brandy decided it was safer for her to be at our hotel than at the clinic with its intermittent electricity and its many typhoid patients. Mostly Brandy slept during this time, but during my shifts I occasionally caught her awake, and she reached out to hold my hand.

On day three after the accident, she told me, "I have a tremendous headache." She asked, "Can you tell me what happened? I can't remember." Thank goodness she didn't remember the fall and cracking her head. But she did remember that I had been there to help.

I told her about her slipping off the trail and my rushing down to see if she was all right. I was initially reluctant to tell Brandy about the role I felt God had played in bringing her back, but finally I said to her, "I felt like God's love was flowing through me. He saved you by giving me clarity and strength. I believe you're alive because God did not want you to go. I believe God saved you so great things will happen to you."

The irony wasn't lost on me that I had been told the same thing many years ago when I had come close to death.

Brandy ended up making a full recovery, and we kept in touch for a while afterward. In an email, she wrote to me, "My whole soul just cried with the realization and memory of how close to death I came and how divinely protected and taken care of I was. It seems like you were led to save my life. I'm just very much in awe."

Rescuing Brandy was a more serious matter than helping the two young women in Cabo. When I reflected on the two incidents, I couldn't help comparing them to my work. Although I sometimes took a lighthearted approach to promoting clean water solutions, I recognized that the consequences of what I was doing were no less serious or urgent than Brandy's fall. Yet in the time since this realization, I have wondered, *How seriously should I be taking myself?*

I have a tendency to rush to the rescue without thinking. This has been good for the people I've helped, but it has also caused difficulties and pain for the people I love the most.

In retrospect, it's not surprising that, while my family was also concerned about Brandy, they felt that once again I had rushed off to rescue others while neglecting them in the process. During the rest of the trip, my attention was always divided, even when I was with my family, because I was worried about Brandy. Even after others stepped in to help care for her, it was hard to be present for my family because now that I had helped to rescue her, I felt responsible for her full recovery. And when I tried to tell my wife about how I felt God's love flowing through me when I was helping Brandy, she was understandably upset. *She* wasn't feeling loved through any of these actions.

In fact, what happened on vacation was a microcosm of the rest of my life. I had been prioritizing water work over the day-to-day responsibility to be present to my wife as a husband and to my daughters as their dad. Dr. Greg Allgood was playing the hero—but at the cost of my relationships at home.

My wife and I didn't talk about this much at the time, but we had been drifting apart because of my frequent absences, and we continued to do so. By the time we sought professional help for our marriage, it was too late, and in 2009, we divorced.

I did some significant soul-searching during that time. The stress of the divorce was tremendous, and I developed illness after illness—normal things, like prolonged colds and the seasonal flu, but also other, uncommon illnesses. An infection in my leg became so severe it was difficult to walk, much less keep up running. I then developed a throat tumor that grew so large it was making it difficult to breathe.

I eventually recovered from these ailments, but there is no doubt that the stress of the divorce and the responsibility I felt for it reduced my immune system and caused my illnesses.

I was feeling desperate, and I prayed for healing, both physically and mentally. I asked God for renewed direction. I had been playing the hero, but I was the one who needed saving. After the valley I had been walking through, I had no idea I would soon meet God on a mountaintop.

11

SUMMIT ON THE SUMMIT

To honor relatives in his homeland of Ethiopia who had suffered from the effects of contaminated water, the musician Kenna conceived the idea of summiting the highest peak in Africa, the 19,341-foot-tall Mount Kilimanjaro in Tanzania. But that's a rough climb, and he abandoned his attempt before making it to the top. Back home in the United States, he told the story of his failure to his friend Justin Timberlake, who suggested that Kenna gather some friends and try again as a group.

Kenna initiated Summit on the Summit: Kilimanjaro in 2010 as an effort to draw attention to the global water crisis and inspire action. It was one of the first major mountain expeditions to fully leverage social media. The celebrities joining the hike included Jessica Biel, Emile Hirsch, Lupe Fiasco, Kick Kennedy, Isabel Lucas, and Santigold. Other participants included Alexandra Cousteau (filmmaker and granddaughter of Jacques Cousteau), mountaineering experts Jimmy Chin and Melissa Arnot, photographer Michael Muller, Elizabeth Gore of the UN Foundation, and renowned trainer Jason Walsh. And *me*.

As part of the cause-marketing effort for the Children's Safe Drinking Water Program, Procter & Gamble financially supported Summit on the Summit: Kilimanjaro, including sponsoring a ninety-minute MTV documentary about the hike. We hoped to get Justin Timberlake to present it, but we knew we'd probably have to involve agents and negotiate, and we weren't sure how best to approach all that.

The launch for the hike took place at a red-carpet event in Los Angeles. Timberlake would not be able to participate in the hike itself because he would be filming *The Social Network*, but he attended the launch party. On a whim, I approached him and his then-girlfriend Jessica Biel and thanked them for their support of the hike.

"Jessica's going," Justin said. "I'm sorry I can't go along myself. But I want to do whatever I can to build awareness of the hike."

"Well," I said, "there might be something you could do. What would you think about presenting the MTV documentary?"

"Sure," he agreed.

Simple as that.

I was nervous about the hike. I was now fifty years old, and most of the other hikers were in their twenties or thirties. I was also the only water scientist and felt that for this reason I had to make it to the top, no matter what it took. I wasn't sure I could make it, so I turned to prayer. I would take whatever help I could get.

I trained hard. I lived near P&G's headquarters in Cincinnati, which isn't known for its mountainous terrain, but I hiked the hills I could find. When the weather turned cold, I ran up and down the stairwells of the seventeen-story P&G twin towers with a backpack holding thirty pounds of weights. I actually passed out on the stairs one day and was glad it was only from exhaustion and not a more serious health issue. Those stairwells were so rarely used, there's no telling how long it would have been before I'd be discovered. As it was, I regained consciousness on my own.

When I arrived in Tanzania, I met Jimmy Chin, who was at the time a world-famous climber and later became a famous filmmaker with films including *Free Solo* and *Nyad*.

"I'd appreciate any guidance you have to help me make it to the top," I told him. "You'll never have a better student, and I'm committed to do whatever you tell me."

Jimmy graciously agreed to help.

The day before we started the seven-day hike, I hosted my fellow hikers on a visit to a Maasai village where we were providing the P&G packets. Our team looked in shock at the shallow, muddy pond where people collected their drinking water. Cows came wading into the pond as some women collected water in their buckets.

Lupe Fiasco, musician and friend of Kenna, could hardly believe that people drank this water. "That's their water source. *That*." He shook his head. "We need to tell people about this. We need to go to Congress and demand action."

As difficult as it was for the team to take in the reality of the problem, they were amazed when they saw a demonstration of the P&G packets and met some of the people who were already using them. It was powerful for them to see up close that we could clean and purify this water, and to see the difference it made for the people in need of it. It strengthened our resolve to spread awareness, both of the water crisis and of solutions.

During the journey, I spent quite a bit of time hiking with Alexandra Cousteau. Jacques Cousteau had passed away over a decade earlier, so getting to know his granddaughter was the next best thing to meeting my childhood hero. I had told my daughters that Alexandra would be part of the hike, and they had advised me to not share with her how much I knew about the Cousteau family because it might appear creepy. So at first I played it cool.

During the miles and miles of hiking, she told me about her grandfather and her own interesting life. I told her stories about my work helping to provide clean water. At one point she looked at me and said, "Greg, you are truly a rock star of water."

For her to say that was mind-blowing and humbling. I had to come clean. "Your grandfather inspired me when I was a teen to study science. I wouldn't be here without him."

Alexandra was touched and shared some stories about growing up with her grandfather as her father figure, since her father had died during one of the Cousteau expeditions when she was little.

I had now come as close as possible to getting to know my two childhood heroes, Jane Goodall and Jacques Cousteau.

As we went along, the hike was much more of a mental challenge than a physical one. On the day we attempted to summit, we slept just a few hours, starting the climb a little after midnight. The best way to deal with the lack of oxygen is to go excruciatingly slowly, putting one foot in front of the other at the count of about one step per second.

Before we set out for the summit, Kenna told us, "Mental baggage prevented me from summiting the first time I tried. Before we go, I want to encourage you to clear your minds. Don't take a lot of mental or emotional stuff with you to the top of the mountain."

I paused as I considered Kenna's challenge. I knew I was still harboring anger and resentment over people who had objected to P&G's not-for-profit effort. As I reviewed the situation in my mind, I tried to let go of bitterness. They'd had logical reasons for their opposition, including not believing I had what it took to lead such an effort. And who could really blame them? I hadn't believed it either before hearing the voice of God.

More importantly, I unloaded some personal baggage. I've made plenty of mistakes in my life, and I regretted the choices I'd made that led to my marriage ending in divorce. I knew I had prioritized my career over my family, feeling like I had to do everything on my own. I had convinced myself that quality time when we were together made up for the times we were apart, but I knew now that wasn't the case.

And it wasn't just my family. It was true even with my close childhood friends, Wes and Don. I almost never connected with them unless I was traveling to North Carolina to see my family. They graciously made time for me even when I gave them only a day's notice that I was rolling into town.

All too often, I had made choices for my career instead of for my family and friends. This had a negative impact on both me and others. I had frequently used the excuse that I was saving lives with my work, but on the mountain, I saw this was a false choice. It wasn't a matter of doing one or the other. I needed to do both and to make my loved ones a priority more often than I had.

I had already sought forgiveness from my family, but when Kenna asked us to leave our mental baggage behind, I realized I hadn't forgiven myself. I was still carrying regret and guilt like they were an extra weight in my pack. I wasn't capable of forgiving myself, so I prayed God would help me to get out from under the burden of what I had done. I felt the Holy Spirit remove my guilt. I was lighter and rejuvenated. I was ready to ascend.

It was a grueling hike, but all our team made it to the top of Kilimanjaro. The average success rate of people attempting to summit Kilimanjaro—the highest mountain in the world routinely hiked without supplemental oxygen—is 50 percent. We believed our 100 percent completion rate was due to our focus on the goal of raising awareness of the global water crisis. We supported, encouraged, and waited for each other.

It was bitterly cold at the summit, freezing the water in our bottles. And so, ironically, on this hike for clean drinking water, we didn't have any water we could drink to refresh ourselves after our exertion. Our photographer took what became the iconic photo of the trip, and we quickly headed down.

The Summit on the Summit was a huge public relations success. It generated over one billion media impressions; it was the number-two trending topic on Twitter during the climb; and the PUR Water Filtration brand signed up fifty thousand Facebook fans in a single day, all of which built the awareness we were going for.

For World Water Day, we did just as Lupe had urged us at the dirty water hole, and our team of climbers went to Washington to advocate for clean water. We were hosted at the US Capitol by Representative Earl Blumenauer from Oregon, the author of the Paul Simon Water for the World Act. The visibility of the Summit on the Summit gave us access to lawmakers that many of us wouldn't have had otherwise.

It also helped build support among government leaders for prioritizing clean water for the world. Both Kenna and I were asked to present, along with a dozen water experts, at the National Geographic Society that World Water Day. Secretary of State Hillary Clinton gave the keynote address at our gathering. She spoke on the role of water as an instrument for peace. "It's not every day you find an issue where effective diplomacy and development will allow you to save millions of lives, feed the hungry, empower women, advance our national security interests, protect the environment, and demonstrate to billions of people that the United States cares, cares about you and your welfare," she said. "Water is that issue."[1]

Many people, including me, had spent years in advocacy with the US government to have this high-level commitment to provide clean water. Everyone in attendance realized how momentous this speech was.

Around this time we also launched the MTV documentary at the Library of Congress and flew to New York for a red-carpet event in New York City. We held a reception at the State Department featuring a photo exhibit of Jimmy Chin's and Michael Muller's photography from the trip.[2]

The Paul Simon Water for the World Act was later signed into law in 2014.

But before any of those follow-up events came to pass, I had another crisis to deal with.

After two days of descending from the top of Mount Kilimanjaro and traveling to our post-hike hotel, I luxuriated in my first shower in a week. As I connected to the Internet to check my messages and see what I'd missed in the news, I learned that—on the same day and at about the same hour that I was standing on the summit of Kilimanjaro—a 7.0-magnitude earthquake had hit Haiti and killed three hundred thousand people. This was a major disaster and was receiving the kind of global attention the southeast Asia tsunami had a few years earlier. I knew there was an immediate need for the P&G packets.

While the rest of the Summit group headed for Ethiopia, I made my way to the Dominican Republic. I had to take an overland route from there into Haiti. I didn't unpack from the Kilimanjaro hike. I even had my sleeping bag with me, because I wasn't sure what kind of lodging I might be able to secure. As it turned out, I was able to share a hotel room in Port-au-Prince with four other relief workers.

During the middle of the first night, I was awakened from deep sleep by an aftershock. My roommates and I gathered in the courtyard to await the all-clear signal, indicating it was safe to head back to our room. We were sharing the hotel with Haitian survivors of the quake, and the tremors were terrifying to them. Even in the moonlight, I could see the fear in their faces and the comfort they were trying to give each other by huddling together. I hoped we could provide some relief for these and other survivors.

This earthquake was worse than any other natural disaster I had ever seen (and by this time, unfortunately, I'd seen quite a few). The destruction went on for fifty miles, with most buildings down. And yet, already in the first week, people were digging out, burying their dead, and doing the things they needed to do to survive. They wanted our help, but they were going to move forward with or without us. The resilience of the Haitian people was truly inspiring.

I was heartbroken to hear that the Hotel Montana had collapsed, killing hundreds of people inside. I visited the site and grew upset as I looked at the rubble that still hid the remains of so many people. It all seemed so *senseless*.

I spent several days interacting with groups who had an interest in using the P&G packets. The coordination of emergency relief efforts had greatly improved since the southeast Asia tsunami, with UNICEF providing a leadership role for the water, sanitation, and hygiene sector. I also visited some of the communities where the packets were already being used and saw that they were providing a much-needed source of clean water.

Many of the other people staying at the hotel with me were emergency room personnel from Canada volunteering with GlobalMedic. During breakfast, I listened to their stories. Despite their being used to dealing with trauma, they seemed almost in a state of shock, as if they'd been in combat. But I found it was more than just the human toll that stunned them.

One member of the Canadian team said, "I've never seen anything like what we're witnessing among these people."

"What do you mean?" I asked. I thought he was probably referring to the extent of the suffering.

"We're doing a lot of amputations on people whose limbs were damaged by falling buildings," he went on, "but we've run out of pain meds and have to do these operations without being able to offer pain relief or anesthesia of any kind. I was expecting these people to scream while we work on them. But do you know what they actually do during the amputations?"

"What?"

"They're praying and singing hymns." Amid the lack of anesthesia and pain medications, the Haitians were seeking the comfort of God.

I've been in lots of disaster situations. But when I encountered peace in the midst of disaster before, I had assumed it was because people's lives were less complicated without the modern demands associated with life in the US or other, richer areas. But hearing the relief workers' stories and seeing firsthand the peace that the Haitian people derived from their faith, I was now able to see how God is present where there is suffering. And I also realized that while so much suffering does seem senseless, God had equipped me to be present and to help in these situations.

God's presence seemed much more tangible in the world's poorest places than I usually experienced at home. And it wasn't just in cases of acute suffering but during all the normal travails that come with poverty. From here on out, I detected God's presence more and more among people living in deep poverty.

Not that God's closeness to the world's needy should ever have been a surprise to me. Jesus taught that we will find him among the poor (see Matthew 25:31-46). That's more than just a theological point. It's a reality. And feeling God's presence is one of the most fulfilling (and humbling) parts of working with people in extreme poverty.

While in Haiti, I recorded a segment to air on *SOS—Saving Ourselves—Help for Haiti*, hosted by Queen Latifah. P&G was a sponsor and asked me to provide footage to encourage people to donate to the relief effort.

Meanwhile, Kenna and Lupe Fiasco wrote, recorded, and released a song and accompanying video called "Resurrection," with proceeds from the song going to help Haitians.[3] (They used a clip of my reporting from Haiti in their video.)

I believe I was able to do some good in Haiti during a terrible time. Through my time there, I began to pay more attention to the places God was at work, to notice God's personal care and compassion for his children in distress.

12

GOODBYE, HELLO

Back when I'd written my "five years from the future" story in 2004, one thing I had forecast was that John Pepper, former Procter & Gamble CEO, would come out of retirement to provide the one billionth liter of clean water. At that time, this vision seemed more like a fantasy than a vision. We'd only provided thirty million liters of water during the three years of the commercial effort. Reaching one billion liters would mean the not-for-profit effort was surely an unrealistic outcome. Yet it happened, and sooner than I expected.

In 2008 we hosted a celebration for this achievement at a clinic in Nigeria, with John Pepper present to mark the occasion. He said in his speech, "This milestone event marks both a humanitarian triumph and a technological achievement. But what really matters is that we are helping to save lives."[1]

We continued to celebrate each billionth liter in a similar way. It was a way to highlight the progress we were making. (As I'm writing this in 2025, P&G has already celebrated twenty-five billion liters of clean drinking water provided by the purification packets.)

Yet even before that first celebration in Nigeria, I felt something was missing in these billion-liter celebrations. The issue was that it was hard to comprehend what a billion liters meant. We translated one billion liters into the number of Olympic-size swimming pools and tanker trucks that could be filled with this much water, but these illustrations lacked the emotional impact I desired. I saw firsthand what a difference clean water meant for *people*, and I wanted others to see this too. For years I chewed on this desire for a better way to express our impact.

Then one day the solution came to me. Based on our desired growth of the program and epidemiological data from the World Health Organization, I calculated we had the potential to provide enough clean water to save about nine thousand lives a year, or about one life every hour. This was an *aha!* moment. I found it difficult to comprehend one billion liters, but I could easily visualize one life by thinking of one of my daughters. I was convinced the idea of "saving one life every hour" was a potential game changer for our program.

On a plane to Washington, DC, to accept the Ron Brown Award for Corporate Leadership in 2007, I traveled with Susan Arnold, the vice chair of P&G, and A. G. Lafley, the CEO. I shared with Susan my idea of ramping up the clean water program so we could "save one life every hour." She was excited by this idea. During our trip, she shared the idea with A. G., and she went even further and told him we needed new manufacturing capacity for the packets to achieve this vision.

This was *not* business as usual.

I'd worked on several projects, and was familiar with many more, in which additional manufacturing capacity was needed. There are feasibility studies, sourcing studies, and many levels of approval needed. It's a lengthy process and usually occurs after the established growth of a product. I'd never heard of a multimillion-dollar manufacturing decision based on a vision statement. But that's what happened in this case. A. G. agreed to Susan's request for funding on the spot.

We waited to announce our goal to provide enough clean water to save one life every hour until we had built the manufacturing capacity. That occurred in 2010. Bob McDonald had by this time become CEO of P&G, and he launched our "save one life every hour" effort at the Clinton Global Initiative annual meeting in 2010 in front of about a thousand world leaders, including heads of state and CEOs from both the for-profit and the not-for-profit worlds.

I can still hear former President Clinton telling the audience, "This is a really big deal."

At the Clinton Global Initiative meeting the following year, in 2011, President Clinton said something else that stuck with me. "If everyone did their part, according to their own abilities, we would easily solve the global water crisis."[2] This was—and is—so true. The water crisis is *solvable*, and its solution will be a great return on investment through the reduction in illness and death and the increased economic opportunities of people freed from hauling water.

President Clinton was speaking to representatives from companies and NGOs when he cast this vision, so he probably was implying that every *organization* should do its part. But I took his words personally. I had discovered my purpose when I met Mercy all those years ago, and as a result I had worked hard to make P&G's Children's Safe Drinking Water Program a success. But I began to think about whether I was doing all I could to help solve the global water crisis. Maybe there was another role where I could accomplish more.

At this point in my life, I'd rarely spent time in deep introspection. In fact, my ambition and focus on achieving the next goal probably caused me to spend *less* time searching for deeper meaning than most people. Besides, I was so busy all the time that just keeping up with what was happening took most of my focus and energy. But the seed that was planted at the Clinton Global Initiative took root in my mind, and I thought about it more and more. Was it time to move on? Potentially leaving the P&G water purification program was a difficult decision, and I needed to consider carefully before taking this step.

Perhaps it was God's doing, but I was almost forced into a time of deep reflection in February 2012. I was visiting CARE's work with the P&G packets in Ethiopia near the Somalia border. It took two long days of car travel to reach the site, my driver didn't speak English, and there was no Internet service, so I couldn't entertain myself with my phone. I had two days of travel to the border and two days of travel back to Addis Ababa to reflect on my life and work. I stared out the window of the Toyota Land Cruiser at a terrain that looked like Mars, with an occasional termite mound rising from the arid red soil. And as I did, I consciously focused on my past and future.

For the quarter century or so of my P&G career, I'd worked extremely hard in my pursuit of success. And one conclusion I reached was that I'd probably have worked just as hard to be successful, and to be *seen* as successful, even if it hadn't been for such a noble cause as providing clean water. That was just in my nature. So I was thankful God had given me this purpose to channel the ambition I'd always had.

Another conclusion? I felt deep ownership of the P&G water program. It seemed like I'd given birth to it, risked my career for it, and devoted much of my life to the cause. It was difficult to think about separating from the program. I had poured so much of myself into it that in some ways it had become my identity. I couldn't really imagine myself apart from my cause.

One time I was talking to Bob McDonald, and he said casually, "We are only shepherds of our work." At the time that didn't sit well with me, and I didn't understand why. Now, left alone with time to reflect, I realized I'd had too much ownership of the program. Too often "Dr. Greg Allgood" had been the hero, and I'd believed the program couldn't survive without me. But if the P&G program was going to continue, it needed to be seen as being much more than me.

As much as I loved my role in the Children's Safe Drinking Water Program and the impact I was able to have, I was beginning to accept that I needed a new calling. I felt that the time was drawing near for retiring from my company and finding something else to do.

I felt this especially keenly when, in connection with a monthly town hall meeting for P&G employees, the personal health care division surprised me with an honor previously reserved for people working within the division. (I'd been under the sustainability group for some time.) They hired a film crew to interview key P&G people and my family in Cincinnati to create a video titled "One Person Can Change the World." I was deeply moved by this honor.

Charlotte Otto, the head of P&G external relations at the time, said, "I've never met anyone who has so much passion for what they do and regularly infects others with his passion."

It felt good to be recognized.

But I felt remorse and regret when my daughter Meredith reflected on the impact my absences had had on our family. "It's very hard when he's away," she said, "but I know why he's doing it. I know he's doing it for others, and it makes it not so hard." Since my time on Kilimanjaro, I had resolved to find a better balance between my work and being there for my kids. While I had succeeded in some regards, I knew this hadn't been representative of my career to this point. I was glad to hear Meredith understood *why* I was doing it, but I recommitted to doing better for my family in the future.

Following the meeting, one of my friends in personal health care joked, "Now you have the video to show at your future retirement celebration!"

I laughed at this, but it further nurtured the thought about my season at P&G coming to an end.

Still, while I was at P&G, I continued to do everything I could to grow the water work.

In 2011 P&G sold off the PUR Water Filtration business. I was worried they might sell off everything with the PUR name, including the packets. But P&G did not sell the PUR water purification packets and agreed to rebrand them with a new name. As part of the sale of the PUR Water Filters, I gained agreement for funds to be used for rebranding the packets.

I proposed to Marc Pritchard, P&G's chief brand officer, that we use the name of the company as the new name of the product—P&G Purifier of Water. This was a bold idea, because we had not named a product with the company name for more than a hundred years. But I argued, "We could more easily build P&G reputation with the packets *and* make the purpose of the company tangible if they have the same name."

Marc readily agreed.

With the funds available for rebranding, we built awareness of the rebranding in the eleven countries providing the packets using the social-market model, and we updated our communication materials with the new name.

There were enough funds remaining to help sponsor a second Summit on the Summit: Kilimanjaro. I was off to make another climb of the tallest peak in Africa.

Kenna, Melissa Arnot, and I were joined this time by musician Mark Foster, actors Beau Garrett and Justin Chatwin, photographer Chase Jarvis, media personality Lauren Sánchez (prior to her marriage to Jeff Bezos), and filmmaker Bryn Mooser. As with the climb three years earlier, I was disciplined in my training. I knew I'd be the oldest in our group—twenty to thirty years older than most. But when we set off for Kilimanjaro, I felt strong—physically, mentally, and spiritually.

For the final ascent, we rose at eleven p.m. We were blessed with a clear sky and could view the stars for hours as we slowly made our way up the mountain. Many of our climbers suffered badly from the altitude, but we stayed together as a group, helping each other up the mountain. My feet were very cold, and I lost feeling in them after the first hour.

I told my fellow climbers, "If we can just make it to sunrise, we'll feel much better." I knew this from the first climb.

The sunrise atop Kili is one of the most beautiful things I've ever seen in nature. This time it was glorious, covering half the horizon as we reached Stella Peak, less than a mile from Uhuru Peak, the top of Mount Kilimanjaro.

Throughout the hike, Kenna encouraged us and reminded us why we were hiking. As we rounded the final bend, we gathered as a group and shouted, "Clean water!" Once again, Summit on the Summit: Kilimanjaro defied the odds by having all the climbers make it to the top.

For me, being on top of the world and looking at the beautiful scene reinforced the deep sense of satisfaction I was feeling about all I had accomplished in my career to that point. So many years had passed since meeting Mercy had revealed to me the life-and-death stakes of clean water for the world's neediest people. Then, when it looked like the water program (and my job along with it) was about to go away, God had asked me, *Do you doubt I can do this?* He had gone on to prove that, with him, a nonprofit cause for clean water was possible for P&G and indeed could be highly successful. It hadn't all been perfect, but as the saying goes, it was "all good."

Long ago, my scout leader Frank Goodrum had told me, "God saved you for a reason. He must have a plan for your life to make a difference." This had already come true. I had already made a difference in the fight for clean water. And what I wanted for the rest of my career was to make even *more* of a difference in this cause. But I felt peace that it didn't have to be at P&G.

On the evening of our final camp, I told Kenna privately, "I'm thinking about retiring from P&G." I was still not comfortable talking about my faith, but based on our friendship, I told him, "I think God is telling me to consider this step."

"Well, if that's the case," he said, "you'd better listen to what God is telling you."

He was right. God *was* telling me it was time to retire from P&G, and I had to listen. And what's more, God was telling me where to go next.

During my years with the Children's Safe Drinking Water Program, I would seek out new partners through a variety of methods. I'd ask our current partners for recommendations, I'd meet representatives of organizations at meetings, and I'd come across them during my visits to developing countries. One of the partners I'd heard a lot about from early on was World Vision.

Based on what I'd seen and heard, I'd concluded quickly that

World Vision would be an excellent partner for P&G. This NGO had a long history and a solid reputation. And importantly, they worked in the toughest-to-reach places, the ones where people typically have the dirtiest water sources. This is the niche for the P&G packets.

In 2007 I met Rich Stearns—at the time the president of World Vision US—while standing in line at an event. Rich was in his late fifties, tall and lean, with a full head of gray hair that gave him a distinguished look. He was both passionate and deeply thoughtful.

Rich asked me, "Has P&G ever considered working with World Vision?"

Now, the truth was that I *had* sought out opportunities to work with World Vision several times but had gained no traction beyond a few small, short-lived efforts. Rich evidently didn't know about any of this. So instead of complaining to him, I played hard to get. "*Should* we work with World Vision?"

In rapid fire, Rich offered a series of reasons for P&G to work with his organization.

I didn't want to seem too eager, so I paused before I said, "You make a good case for collaboration. I'd be interested in discussing it more."

He took my business card. "World Vision will be in touch with you soon."

Within World Vision, the P&G partnership was assigned to Keith Kall. Keith and I agreed we should gain experience in one country, monitor the effort closely, and then share our experience with other World Vision offices. We picked Malawi and executed the plan to perfection. The P&G–World Vision partnership grew exponentially from there. Within a few years, World Vision was one of our partners using the most P&G packets.

I was able to visit World Vision's work with Keith in a dozen countries. I was impressed when I was able to return to the same community after a few years and see the transformation in development. People were going from barely surviving in extreme poverty to now thriving. They were going from high rates of illness, poor school attendance, poor nutrition, and lack of time for women to earn a living because of hauling water every day, to healthy and vibrant communities. Clean water was the basis for this transformation.

World Vision used the P&G packets as one small but important part in a holistic effort to help people climb out of poverty. The best approach was when World Vision used the packets on an interim basis prior to providing a permanent water source, usually accomplished by digging a borehole with a drilling rig and installing a hand pump.

I was extremely impressed with World Vision staff. They sacrificially worked and even lived in the remote communities they served. Some people would call this local presence "boots on the ground," but based on their Christian faith, World Vision staff preferred to call it "sandals in the sand," reminding them of Jesus. People in the communities trusted World Vision staff, and World Vision staff loved the poor and loved serving them.

Of course, trust is earned over time. The commitment of the World Vision staff to these communities earned them trust. The introduction of a new product, such as the P&G packets, was much more successful when provided by trusted hands. I was able to witness this success, and we grew our partnership as a result. In fact, of all the capable partners I had worked with, I felt World Vision was doing the best job in helping to solve the global water crisis. I could see myself being on their team.

Once I had made the decision to retire from P&G, I contacted World Vision about my interest in working with them and eventually agreed to take a position of leadership in their water work. Here, I hoped and believed, was the opportunity I was looking for to make a bigger impact on the world's water crisis.

Prior to my retirement announcement, P&G management asked me to visit many of our P&G locations around the world to tell the story of how one person was able to have a tremendous impact. This trip took place in May 2013, a month before my retirement. I was proud to meet P&Gers in Cairo, Costa Rica, Dubai, Nairobi, Geneva, and Singapore, as well as in Cincinnati, to share my story. The trip gave me a deep sense of satisfaction in what I had accomplished for the company.

In my final blog post for P&G, I told readers I'd been truly blessed to work there. I'd been to areas hit by tsunamis, earthquakes, floods, cholera outbreaks, drought, and famine. I'd wept with people who had buried their children and their spouses because of waterborne illness and was thankful I'd continue efforts to help address the global water crisis in my new position.

I concluded like this:

> I love the quote from Bob Pierce, the Founder of World Vision, who said, "Let our hearts be broken by the things that break the heart of God." My heart has been broken many times by what I've witnessed, and I've learned that Bob Pierce prayed this because this breaking of the heart is actually a tremendous gift. It breaks through the complacency that comes with our privileged lives and allows us to focus on what really matters. The breaking of the heart allows us to grow an even greater capacity to love.
>
> Through these experiences, I've learned that our efforts make a difference. Not only do we restore hope in those we help, but we gain immensely in a sense of purpose in our own lives. This fulfillment and sense of purpose allows us to do amazing things. Things that we could never envision without this motivation.[3]

13

VICE PRESIDENT OF WATER

"I don't know what the question is yet, but the answer is yes," Chris Glynn, the senior vice president at World Vision, told me while I was sitting in his office.

"What's that?" I said. "I'm afraid I don't understand."

This was in early 2013, after I had decided to retire from Procter & Gamble and seek a position at World Vision. I was meeting some of the World Vision senior leaders for interviews at their headquarters in Federal Way, Washington. I liked all of them and felt the interviews were going well, but Chris Glynn had stumped me with his "the answer is yes" comment.

"What I mean," he said, "is that we may need some time to figure out where you'll best fit within World Vision. But as far as I'm concerned, I want you to join us."

Eventually Chris created a new role for me as vice president of water, reporting directly to him. Chris envisioned my role as marketer as well as subject matter expert who would help build World Vision's reputation as a leader in water and work with the technical team to set the strategy for World Vision's water, sanitation, and hygiene efforts. One of my key tasks would be helping World Vision raise funds for the work—something I had no experience in but was eager to learn about.

I was fifty-four when I switched from P&G to World Vision in the summer of 2013. I figured I had about eighteen years left in my career. Although I felt good about all I had done at P&G to combat the global water crisis, I wanted to make the most of the productive years I had left. I felt a renewed sense of urgency in my calling. Working at World Vision would enable me to help people gain clean water in more comprehensive ways than I had before since I would be part of a much larger team and working in many more of the world's neediest areas.

In order to start at World Vision with maximum energy and freshness, I planned to take the summer off between retiring from one job and starting the other. I bought a house in Boulder, Colorado, and moved all my belongings from Cincinnati. Even though the World Vision headquarters is in the Seattle area, I would be able to work remotely, and I loved Boulder. Between jobs, I would give myself the first really substantial break I'd had since starting at P&G twenty-seven years prior. I would explore my new area, spend time with friends and my daughters, and arrange my new home the way I liked it.

Well, that didn't happen.

Within a week of settling into my new home in Boulder—while technically employed by no one—I received a call from former President Bill Clinton's team. The president and his daughter, Chelsea, were planning a trip to Rwanda and wanted to include a stop where they could observe the P&G water purification packets in the field. This would mean visiting a World Vision site, since World Vision was the main distributor of packets in that country.

I didn't think about not being an official employee at that moment but jumped right into the planning. After a week of doing this on a volunteer basis, I got a call from Chris Glynn, who suggested I just move up my start date. When President Clinton arrived in Rwanda in early August, I was there as a World Vision leader to greet him.

The advance team had told us that President Clinton and the group traveling with him would spend only twenty minutes with us and would not have time to wait for the packets to fully disinfect the water we would treat. The team also cautioned us not to ask either of the Clintons to drink the treated water. But the president had other plans. Not only did he wait to drink the treated water, but he also instructed everyone in his group to take turns stirring the water in the buckets we had set up for demonstration.

The Rwanda trip was a wonderful way to start my work in building visibility for World Vision's water efforts. It was also gratifying to see my successor at P&G, Allison Tummon Kamphuis, stepping effectively into her new role as the leader of the program. As for myself, since my new role started with such promise, I expected things were only going to get better at World Vision. I was full of confidence. What could go wrong?

The year before, when I was still at P&G, a leading cause marketer (and fellow Boulder resident) David Clark, the CEO of David Clark Cause, had helped me organize a publicity campaign for the fall annual meeting of the Clinton Global Initiative. It was called Smoke Alarm because David had secured the participation of iconic musician Smokey Robinson as the centerpiece.

For 2013, David and I had planned an even larger event, this time called Flash Flood for Good. P&G was the sponsor of the initiative, with World Vision highlighted as the chosen recipient of funds raised. Building on the previous year's success, we were able to secure the endorsements of a wide range of A-list celebrities.

Not long after I had returned from Rwanda, and less than two weeks before the launch of Flash Flood for Good, my new hometown of Boulder experienced two consecutive days of torrential rains. On the second evening, warnings went out about the possible flooding of Boulder Creek. But while I was worried about the safety of others in my community, I was more than a mile from the creek and had no concerns about my own home flooding.

For some reason, that night, as the rain pelted outside, I spent a couple of hours in the basement going through picture albums. It had been only six weeks since I'd moved from Cincinnati to Boulder, and so perhaps moving the albums and putting them on shelves in my new basement spurred this trip down memory lane. This was probably the first time in my life I'd spent so long looking at photos.

Finally, I cut the lights and walked up the two flights of stairs to my bedroom and fell asleep.

About two a.m., I woke to the sound of running water.

I ran down the stairs, but before I could reach the basement, my feet were splashing in water. Water was pouring in from the window well and was already halfway to the ceiling. I noticed something floating on the surface of the water and saw that it was the clump of pictures I'd been looking at earlier that evening. They were ruined, and I would never be able to enjoy them again.

I grabbed a shovel and worked until daylight digging up my yard to create a dam that would divert water from my home. That morning, I hired a group of guys to start pumping the water from my basement. The dam seemed to be holding, and my workers were successful in pumping out most of the water.

But then the rain started again—with a vengeance. Soon the creek was overwhelming my homemade dam, despite my now having some friends' help with sandbagging to reinforce the barrier.

I learned that a three-foot wall of water had flowed from nearby Mount Sanitas and all the homes on my street had been flooded. On the street running parallel to mine, two teenagers who were outside at the time of the flood were swept away and drowned. This was a 750-year flood, and more than a thousand homes were destroyed.

As the rain continued, police were driving through the neighborhood with loudspeakers, telling people to evacuate. In tears, I told the guys pumping out my basement to give up and seek shelter. I opened my front and back doors so the water could flow out of the ground floor as the basement overflowed. I spent the night with a friend.

When I returned early the next morning, the rains had finally stopped. The creek running through my house had reduced to a trickle. Opening the doors had been a good move, because water had flowed out the ground floor like I'd hoped. The basement, however, had worked like a settling tank. Once it was pumped out again, I found two feet of mud. I couldn't help but think of the parallels to the dirt that would collect at the bottom of a water container when using the P&G packets.

I spent the next week hauling stuff out of the basement and salvaging what I could. Several people showed up to help.

I had been to many disaster areas during my emergency relief work with the P&G packets. I always wondered how survivors felt when people showed up for short periods to help out. Being on the receiving end helped me understand how much people appreciate almost any aid efforts, and especially the comfort that comes from knowing someone else sees and cares.

Nevertheless, I entered a deep depression. I was working every daylight hour to extract my possessions from the mud. I had no electricity and no hot water. My hands and arms had cuts from broken glass, and I worried about infection. I'd cover my cuts with

Neosporin every evening, fall asleep exhausted, then wake at daylight to recover more from the mud.

I tried telling myself over and over that these were just material possessions and most of them could be replaced. I still had the most important things in my life—my family, my friends, my health, and my mission to provide clean water. Somehow, though, I couldn't shake a feeling of defeat. I felt just the opposite of the blue-eyed prince.

A friend took a picture of me that I sent to my kids and to some friends. Several commented that they'd never seen me look so dejected. Don and Wes saw how broken I looked and made plans to fly out and help. I appreciated their support, but I told them there was no need to come. I had no place for them to stay and would have to hire professionals to do the rest of the work anyway.

Left to my own thoughts, I wondered if I should give up and just walk away. I felt so low, I didn't even know what to pray for.

I had a flight already scheduled for New York for the launch of Flash Flood for Good (a name that now had a deeper, more ironic meaning for me) at the Clinton Global Initiative and decided I might as well go. If nothing else, the hotel room with its hot shower held more appeal than my dark, damp house.

I went through the motions at the Clinton Global Initiative and tried not to think about all the work ahead of me to recover from the flood. It would take months before my house was comfortable to live in again.

A month after the flood, I flew to North Carolina to attend a scientific conference. While I was there, I made sure to get together with Don and Wes. Before I moved to Boulder, I had seen Don and Wes for a weeklong kayaking trip, an annual reunion I suggested after my time on Kilimanjaro. We had plenty of time to talk, and I had shared with them about my move and about how I thought it might be time to think about marriage again.

Now, when I had dinner with these old friends, they comforted me but also counseled me to ease up a bit.

Wes said, "You've been through a lot, Greg. You just moved across the country from Cincinnati to Boulder, and you are onboarding in your new job, which will be quite a challenge. And we can see that the flood was traumatic for you."

Don laid into me. "Greg, you need to slow down. Spend some time in reflection for a change."

Don, always perceptive, knew I had a tendency to leap before I looked. I had asked him and Wes for advice about dating. "The last thing you need at this point in your life is to start a new relationship. Give it a rest, man."

After Don finished lecturing me, he took a sip of his drink, thought for a few seconds, and then said, "I know you. You're not going to listen to any of this."

Don *did* know me. I always have my eye on the next challenge, and the way I tend to deal with pain is to push through to the next thing.

I had not told these friends that I'd signed up for the dating service eharmony earlier that day or that I'd already had a promising response to my profile. Nor did I tell them now. I only smiled my best enigmatic smile.

After dinner, I snuck off on my own and had my first call with Elaine.

At this point in my life, after my divorce four years earlier, I knew myself. I had resolved that I would better prioritize family, and I meant it. But I also knew that if a new relationship was going to work, I had to lay all my cards on the table from the start. In my profile, I was very clear about who I am and about what I was looking for in a potential mate.

Elaine was intrigued. And after our two-hour conversation, I was too.

Elaine had an adventurous spirit and a straightforward way of communicating. She was very candid with me about what she was looking for and who was important in her life. She loved her two adult children fiercely, and I knew she would not accept excuses when it came to prioritizing family.

Despite her living in St. Louis, despite my starting a new job and settling in to a new hometown and dealing with the aftermath of a flood, we decided to give dating a try.

Elaine and I were later married in 2016.

One of my early recommendations after joining World Vision was to create a sub-brand of World Vision called World Vision Water so we could more readily establish our reputation in water. I had done something similar with brands I worked with at P&G and with the Children's Safe Drinking Water Program, and it had been effective. It showed we were serious and knowledgeable in the areas we were entering.

I'd naively—and perhaps arrogantly—thought I'd be given carte blanche at World Vision in branding and communication. I learned, however, that part of the CEO's leadership team was dead set against the idea of a sub-brand.

We discussed it during a meeting in Seattle.

"I can appreciate your enthusiasm for your area, Greg," one of the leaders said. "But you're new here. What you need to remember is that child sponsorships bring in far more revenue for our work than donations for water. We've had a decline in sponsorships lately. Our priority now should be building visibility of the parent brand to revitalize child sponsorships."

"There's no reason we can't promote World Vision Water and World Vision at the same time," I argued.

"It will be a distraction and confuse our donors."

Heads nodded.

I made my case, pointing out examples from my time at P&G as well as from other groups like the Gatorade Sports Science Institute, which had successfully become known in sports nutrition. Others gave their reasons for keeping water a lower priority. The meeting was animated, with voices raised on both sides.

At one point, the person who was most opposed to the sub-brand insisted that I alter my business card. I had ordered cards that read "Vice President, World Vision Water." The other leader wanted me to remove "World Vision Water" because he didn't believe there should be any such division within our organization.

I had support from the CFO and Chris Glynn, but we weren't making any headway against the others. The meeting ended without a decision.

Following this discussion, I was frustrated. I had hoped the outcome would be like the boardroom decision at P&G where A. G. Lafley had given me approval to move ahead. Instead, there was no resolution. I didn't understand what would happen next. Did I really have a job with World Vision if there was no consensus on what I was doing?

I was left dangling, and I began to doubt that I would have the impact I'd hoped for here.

Early in 2014 I left for a trip to Africa to see more of World Vision's water efforts. This was a multiweek trip starting in Ghana, then moving on to Senegal, and winding up in Mali.

I was already in discomfort from an unprovoked moray eel bite

I'd sustained near Christmas—the first time an eel had bitten me in over one thousand hours of diving. But during the Mali portion of the trip, I began to have a hard time focusing. I developed flu-like symptoms, including fever, nausea, headache, and extreme tiredness. By the last day of our field visits, I was having a difficult time getting out of our jeep to visit the villages where World Vision was providing water wells. Kathryn Compton, another World Vision leader, was also on the trip and was experiencing similar symptoms.

When we got back to Bamako, the capital, she arranged for a local doctor to meet us at our hotel. He diagnosed our affliction as malaria and gave us medication. My symptoms improved, and I thought I had fully recovered.

Then a few weeks later, during a trip to Washington, DC, the symptoms I had experienced in Mali returned with a vengeance. I was so fatigued that it took all my strength to visit an emergency room, where, again, they gave me malaria medication.

I recovered, only to suffer a third bout of symptoms soon afterward. By this point I was having difficulty walking up the stairs in my home. One time I bent over, and a liter of fluid drained from my lungs.

I asked my colleagues at the Centers for Disease Control to help me find a physician specializing in tropical medicine. This specialist confirmed I had pneumonia and an antibiotic-resistant malaria. With the proper medications, I was able to recover in a few months.

I've become sick many times during my travels, but this was the worst it ever got. I felt miserable and had a hard time enjoying my new job or my new relationship with Elaine. I fell to brooding.

During the first several months at World Vision, my home was devastated by a 750-year flood, I faced stiff resistance in using my tried-and-true approaches to build visibility of World Vision's water program, I took an eel bite to my hand, and I contracted both pneumonia and antibiotic-resistant malaria. Were these signs? I began to wonder if I had made the wrong decision in joining World Vision.

It wasn't all green lights when I discovered my purpose and worked to start the nonprofit effort at P&G, but now that I'd already come so far, I expected God to use me in even bigger ways. I thought my time of struggling toward my calling was over. But everything in this season was harder than I'd imagined it would be. I didn't know if I was going to be able to have the impact in bringing people clean water that I wanted. Maybe this second phase of my career hadn't been such a good idea after all.

I'd always thought I would eventually retire to a home in my beloved North Carolina. Now I was thinking, *Maybe I should head out there sooner rather than later.*

I was in a dark mood, and my time with World Vision could have ended right there. But during this brooding, I also couldn't stop thinking about a surprising fact I'd learned during my onboarding.

On one of my early trips to the World Vision headquarters in Seattle, I joined a meeting of our water team. One of our water donors, Mark Ratley, was also attending. Before we broke for lunch, Mark said grace.

One thing he said during this prayer caught my attention. "And God, thank you for answering our prayers by bringing Greg to World Vision."

As we got in line for a buffet lunch, I asked Mark if he meant anything specific by his prayer.

"Don't you know about the list?"

I shook my head.

"When our leadership made a commitment to grow World Vision's efforts in water," Mark explained, "they realized they needed someone to lead marketing, strategy, and communications. So they made a short list of people well known in the water world. You were on the list, Greg. Then we began praying over the list. So when you called with interest in joining World Vision, it was a direct answer to our prayers."

I got goose bumps. I thought coming to World Vision had been *my* idea. For me to call, seemingly out of the blue, in response to their prayers seemed miraculous to me. And it encouraged me to believe that perhaps, just as God had helped me find an unlikely path forward at P&G, I could make it through this rough period at World Vision and go on to have the impact I hoped for.

I decided to keep at it.

I also never changed my business card. It still reads "Vice President, World Vision Water."

14

TURNING UP THE FLOW

World Vision is the world's largest Christian development and relief organization. It was founded in 1950 by Robert Pierce as a service organization to provide care for children in Korea. By the time I joined in 2013, World Vision was working in about a hundred countries and had thirty-five thousand staff, most of them local to the countries where we worked.

World Vision addresses poverty using a comprehensive, community-based model. Staff live and work in communities, often for twelve years or more, laboring alongside local residents to do whatever is needed so they can lift themselves out of poverty. That typically means improving education, health, and livelihoods, and many times it involves addressing water, sanitation, and hygiene.

Even though there never was a formal decision to establish World Vision Water as a division, I acted like it existed and used that term anyway. I jumped right in to simplify and focus the messaging about World Vision's water work.

I was encouraged by our top fundraiser, Sam Jackson, to try to better understand the heritage of the organization and particularly the history surrounding the water program. After all, World Vision had been doing water work for decades before I joined, and I knew my efforts would be standing on the shoulders of many talented people who came before me. One of these people and my primary instructor in this learning project was Dr. Emmanuel Opong, who had been with World Vision for more than twenty-five years, mostly helping to provide clean water in Africa. He had been a strong advocate for expanding the use of the P&G packets within World Vision, so I already knew him well. It was a pleasure to have him now as a teacher.

In my time at Procter & Gamble, I'd seen many failed water projects—so many that I sometimes wondered if there was any long-term gain in trying to provide water access in remote areas. But it was different in areas where World Vision worked: The interventions seemed to last, and communities seemed to be thriving. How was that possible? Emmanuel Opong knew the answer.

A Ghanaian, Emmanuel will tell you he's just a village boy, but he's also a bright, well-educated guy with natural compassion and love for the poor. He was a nurse when he first started working with World Vision. Emmanuel taught me how important it is to listen to the needs of the community. He was the perfect choice when the organization wanted someone to develop a community engagement model for working more effectively with towns and villages in establishing sustainable water points.

A water point is simply a place where people can get clean water. Emmanuel explained that World Vision determines the type of water point to provide in a community based on an assessment of what will be most sustainable and cost-effective, given the available water sources. Types of water points may include a water kiosk in a community, a hand-pump well, or a solar-powered system. The water may be provided through a borehole drilled by a drilling rig or by a water source (such as a protected spring) and a piped water system running into a community. Each water system is either protected or treated to ensure it is safe for users to drink.

World Vision's minimum standard is to ensure that every community member has access to water within thirty minutes of their home, round trip, including the waiting time at the water point. In more recent years, we've designed the systems so community members can access water directly at their homes. This means that the number of water points in a specific area will vary by population and geography. On average, we estimate about two to three hundred people are served by each water point. Depending on the yield, therefore, many thousands of people can be served by one complete system.

Providing a water point in a remote area is a challenging goal. But in a way, getting the water flowing is the easy part. *Keeping* it flowing is the hard part.

Emmanuel Opong explained the community engagement model he promoted to keep these water points running.[1]

First, Emmanuel reminded me that World Vision uses a holistic approach of not only providing clean water, if that is needed, but also providing improved health care and economic opportunities and ensuring women have a voice in communities so that relationships are improved. Throughout this long-term engagement, World Vision responds to the needs and expressed desires of the community and does not force solutions on them. Instead, World Vision works with the community to help them take ownership over anything brought to them. This includes a new water delivery system.

"World Vision encourages each community that will be getting a water point to select a water committee made up of respected community members," Emmanuel explained. "The water committee will be responsible for collecting small fees from users of the water point. The fund that is built up in this way is designated to pay for maintenance and repairs. So when a pump or other part of the system breaks down, nobody is looking around for World Vision to fix the problem. There are already people there who know what to do and have the resources to get the repairs performed quickly."

In company with Emmanuel, I talked to members of water committees and observed how they handled money and dealt with problems that cropped up with their water points. I can tell you that the World Vision approach results in a totally different attitude compared to what you might find in other places.

When I visit areas where World Vision works, I often ask, "Whose water point is this?"

I've never heard people say, "It's World Vision's water point."

They always tell me, "It's *our* water point."

An unpublished assessment by World Vision had indicated that the model developed by Emmanuel and others resulted in better-than-average sustainability of World Vision water points. So before I even joined, the organization knew they were going in the right direction. But now we needed stronger evidence to measure our success and become recognized as a world water leader.

I met with my friend and colleague Dr. Jamie Bartram, who had moved from the World Health Organization to become the director of the Water Institute at my alma mater, the University of North Carolina–Chapel Hill. I explained what I saw as the need for a well-conducted study to examine the functionality of World Vision water points over time.

He looked at me quizzically. "You don't know about the Hilton-funded study?"

I did not.

Jamie explained how the Conrad N. Hilton Foundation had agreed to fund a study looking at the long-term sustainability of water points and how UNC was a research partner in this work. This study was then in progress.

When UNC and the Hilton Foundation shared the results, we learned there was enough of a sample size to statistically compare water points provided by World Vision with those provided by other organizations.[2] Unfortunately, the study showed that the functionality of water points not provided by World Vision was as reported previously—the older the water point, the more likely it would not be functioning. There was a high rate of water points no longer flowing. For World Vision–provided water points, however, the study showed (almost miraculously) that there was practically *no impact of age*. World Vision water points functioned at a high level whether the water point was two years old or twenty years old.

The study results showed the reason for the superior performance of World Vision water points: water committees. There was no difference in the rate of breakdown of World Vision–provided water points versus others. The World Vision water points were just repaired more quickly because the water committees had collected funds in advance to cover the costs.

In other words, the key factor in sustainable water points wasn't the "hardware" of the type of pump or the hydrology. It was the "software" of community engagement. Emmanuel's community engagement approach was validated by strong science.

When these results were shared, one of the Hilton team members admitted in a private conversation that it was true World Vision water points had better sustainability. He added, "But I think World Vision is sort of cheating in this respect."

"What do you mean?" I asked, taken aback.

"Well, unlike most water NGOs, World Vision's holistic model of development, partly funded by child sponsorship, means you can have a longer presence in communities," he explained. "Water NGOs can't afford to have the same long-term presence in a community as World Vision."

I told my Hilton Foundation colleague, "If that's cheating, then we're guilty."

Community engagement produced local ownership of water points. It also gave me the last bit of encouragement I needed to feel ownership of my role in World Vision's water work. This was the larger purpose I had been searching for. I was involved in a rare and special thing—a water program that really changed things for people.

A few years before I joined, World Vision committed itself to growing its impact in delivering clean water in the developing world. This effort led eventually to the organization creating a position for me as the vice president of water. But prior to that, it led to the creation of World Vision's first business plan for water.

One of World Vision's long-term donor couples, Dave and Dana Dornsife, were foundational to this effort. Dave is chairman of a steel corporation, and he and his wife are some of the most influential philanthropists in the United States, long having made World Vision one of their chief partners. In one of their trips to West Africa, Dave and Dana learned that some of World Vision's staff they'd known for years were looking for new jobs. World Vision water projects then depended heavily on government and foundation grants, and a grant cycle was coming to an end, which would result in needing to let people go. As a successful businessman, Dave knew finding talented and committed personnel is paramount to success, and World Vision's impact would suffer with this loss of people. World Vision needed a longer-term strategy.

In 2010 the Dornsifes committed to providing an astonishing $35 million investment in World Vision's water program based on the five-year business plan developed through this process. The Dornsifes required a comprehensive report and review of the program every six months and would send the next installment of funds based on a successful review as well as on World Vision showing we had secured an equal investment from other donors.

The truth is, World Vision—like most NGOs and ministries—needs donations of all sizes. We know from the story of the widow's mite that Jesus has high respect for small donations given from a heart filled with devotion (see Luke 21:1-4). And small donations can have a big impact. For every fifty-dollar donation, World Vision can provide a person with a sustainable clean water source that transforms their life. One of the ways that World Vision raises funds for our water work is through Team World Vision events. One of their premier events is the Global 6K held every May for which people walk or run the average distance an African woman and girl walks daily for water, and the participants seek financial support from their family and friends. The Global 6K has thousands of participants and raises more than one million dollars each year. We treasure these gifts.

At the same time, if the global water crisis is going to be solved, there's no getting around that it will cost hundreds of millions of dollars. It will take medium- and high- as well as low-figure donors to achieve this goal. And small-gift donors will get the maximum impact when their gifts are combined with those from large donations.

Prior to developing the first five-year business plan, World Vision was reaching about two hundred thousand people with clean water every year. When I joined World Vision midway through this business plan, World Vision was nearing the milestone of one million people reached per year. And we expected bigger and bigger things to come, thanks to ambitious dreams and smart strategies for achieving them.

My part in all this was to raise visibility and focus our efforts.

World Vision was disappointed when some surveys were published showing awareness of water NGOs in the United States. In one study, World Vision was ranked fourteenth out of fifteen in a survey published by Philanthropedia identifying NGOs doing outstanding work in water.[3] World Vision leadership and the Dornsifes knew this needed to change if we were going to continue to grow in impact. Donors want to be confident their money is going toward work that makes a difference, which is why we needed to turn the spotlight on the good work we were already doing. This was one of the reasons World Vision started praying for someone to lead the strategy and marketing efforts—the prayer that (to my continuing amazement) led me to World Vision.

To directly address recognition of World Vision's water impact, we commissioned a study with the accounting firm KPMG to determine the impact of the leading water NGOs. Thirty-seven organizations responded to the survey, including all the top water NGOs. The results showed that World Vision accounted for *37 percent* of people reached with clean water in developing countries in 2013.[4] So even though Philanthropedia had listed us as fourteenth out of fifteen in overall impact, we were actually providing more clean water than any of the other water NGOs.

With these survey results, we added a powerful new message to our arsenal: "World Vision is the leading NGO provider of clean water in the developing world." It was a true statement then, and it is still true today.

My next strategic choice was to set a goal for even bigger impact and to have a rallying effort for our team as well as our donor partners. I wanted something that would have a similar impact to the goal established for the P&G Children's Safe Drinking Water Program of "saving one life every hour." I worked with Sean Kerrigan, then the senior director of World Vision's water team, to align on a plan to ramp up our work.

Based on our footprint at the time in the fourteen countries that were part of our five-year plan, we estimated there were fifty million people in the areas where we worked lacking clean water access. We set a stretch goal to reach everyone, everywhere we worked with clean water in these countries by 2030. When I did the math, I realized that to reach fifty million people by 2030, we needed to increase our impact from the current level of reaching one new person with clean water every *thirty* seconds to reaching one new person every *ten* seconds.

We announced our new goals in New York City the same week the United Nations Sustainable Development Goals were adopted.[5] Goal 6 is to end the global water and sanitation crisis, and not only was World Vision saying we were aligned with this goal, but we were the only NGO laying out a blueprint for how we were going to help achieve it. In addition to our commitment to reach thirty million people by 2030, as an interim goal we committed to reach twenty million people by 2020.

The leading NGO provider of clean water in the developing world.

Targeting the goal of reaching one new person with clean water every ten seconds.

These were bold—and legitimate—claims we could make about our work.

Forbes later ran an article titled "Big Bet Philanthropy: How More Givers Are Spending Big and Taking Risks to Solve Society's Problems." The writer focused much of this article on the Dornsifes and their generosity with World Vision.[6] It showed how World Vision was becoming recognized as arguably the best place to invest if you wanted to help solve the world's water crisis.

Now we just needed to ratchet up the work to meet our ambitious goals.

And we needed to celebrate our accomplishments along the way.

The magic moment for the P&G packets is when water is transformed from dirty to clean, and it didn't take me long to understand that the magic moment for World Vision's water work is when clean water access reaches a village for the first time. I was amazed we didn't have good footage of a water celebration within World Vision. So in 2014 I went to Ghana with a World Vision videographer, and we captured water erupting fifty feet into the air and people dancing in celebration. I joined in the celebration myself, getting soaked as water rained down from the new borehole provided by our drilling rig. This was the first of many times we captured this special moment to inspire donors that their investment was making a difference in people's lives.[7]

During most of these celebrations, people would tell us things like "What our village needed beyond anything else was access to clean water" or "This water is an answer to our prayers!"

But once an older woman asked me, "How did you get the water under the ground?"

"The water was always there," I explained. "We just tapped into an underground source by drilling into it."

She looked at me, shocked and with great frustration. "I've been hauling water all my life," she said. "So have my daughters. And now so are my granddaughters. If water was there all the time, why did it take until now for us to have it?"

I was taken aback by her directness and didn't know quite what to say. Stuttering a bit, I apologized for how long it had taken.

But her comment struck my heart. She was absolutely right to be frustrated. *I* was frustrated as well. Why *was* it taking so long for hundreds of millions of people like her to have clean water? I still believed we needed to celebrate our wins—but we also had to stay focused and keep working toward the larger goal of clean water for everyone.

STRONG WOMEN

When I first joined World Vision, I was wary about raising funds from private donors. Who was I to encourage them to give their wealth to World Vision? I quickly learned that World Vision was providing a bridge to enable people with resources to assist the neediest people in the world, and that was just what it would take to ensure there would be more and more celebrations of new, clean water sources in poor areas all around the world.[1]

I already knew World Vision was an excellent steward of resources, as I'd vetted them myself through my work at Procter & Gamble. I knew that World Vision field staff were some of the most capable and professional development people I'd ever met. I knew that the World Vision model worked to lift people sustainably out of poverty. My role was not to do a "sales job" to separate people from their money. Instead, it was to give them the opportunity to invest well to save lives.

The big surprise I had in working with radically generous private donors was how much I could learn about listening to God and following him by being with them.

Major donor Lani Dolifka has had as much impact as almost anyone on both the work of World Vision and my own spiritual journey. With Lani, I would share a transformative moment when she met another remarkable woman, from the other side of the world. But first I had to get to know Lani myself.

The P&G-sponsored Flash Flood for Good campaign in 2013, which followed Smoke Alarm, far exceeded our expectations. But P&G decided not to continue this effort after my retirement. I tried to interest World Vision in sponsoring the event, but the budgets of NGOs are not as large as those of for-profit companies, and there wasn't money for this outreach. I needed to tell David Clark we wouldn't have a third iteration of the campaign.

Since David and I both lived in Boulder, I suggested we meet to catch up. We gave each other updates on our professional and personal lives. I knew I needed to tell David that our collaboration was unfortunately coming to an end. I took a sip of my drink before giving him the bad news.

Before I could speak, though, David said, "I just met an exceptional person you might like to know, Greg. Her name is Lani Dolifka. She and her husband founded a company that provides low-cost and safe water to underserved communities in the United States through water kiosks. I've talked to her about the amazing work you and World Vision do. She might be interested in funding efforts to provide clean water in the developing world."

"I'd definitely like to meet her."

"She lives nearby," David said. "I'll set up a meeting."

When I think back on that afternoon, I realize that if I had spoken before David did, that would have redirected the conversation, and he probably would not have told me about Lani. I was a sip away from losing the opportunity! God works in mysterious ways.

A week later, I met Lani at the St. Julien Hotel in Boulder, and we hit it off immediately. Lani is soft-spoken but firm. She is respectful and caring. My colleague Kathryn Compton, who later got to know Lani well, describes her as a "soft, warm light" because her calmness and love of humanity shine through in every interaction.

By the end of this first meeting, Lani agreed to become a World Vision donor. She also asked to travel to Africa to see the work. "I need to kick the tires."

Borrowing from my experiences at P&G, I suggested a cause-marketing program to Lani. Right out of the gate, she agreed to an effort where one gallon of water would be donated in the developing world through World Vision for every gallon of water purchased at her company's water kiosks. In the first year alone, this effort donated more than one hundred million gallons of clean water.

My meeting with Lani was not a typical meeting with a prospective donor. She was ready to make a dramatic difference—and fast. I wasn't surprised she was so successful in business.

During our first meeting, I recommended we travel to Kenya so Lani could meet Naomi Nalokae, a woman who had been the subject of a recent video I had helped produce.[2]

The World Health Organization estimates that in sub-Saharan Africa alone women and girls spend cumulatively two hundred million hours *every day* hauling water.[3] Hauling water is backbreaking work, with a single twenty-liter water container weighing about forty-four pounds. I've carried water weighing this much for several miles, and

I can testify that it is exhausting. The opportunity cost in what these women and girls are *not* able to do while in the arduous effort of gathering water is incalculable.

We wanted to create a video showing how the lives of women can be changed when they no longer have to haul water every day, and we decided to do it in Kenya.

I saw Naomi coming to the water point to collect water. She walked with self-confidence and had a wonderful smile, and I knew she would be perfect for our video. I asked her if she would be willing to share her story, and she agreed.

Naomi was a young Maasai woman with three children. She was just twenty-eight years old, the same age as my oldest daughter. She used to walk seven hours a day to collect water, prior to World Vision providing a permanent water source just a few minutes' walk from her home. She had to do this every single day for her family to have water. (Naomi told me her mother had actually given birth to her on one such water walk.) I was amazed at her strength.

Now that Naomi has clean water near her house, her life has changed dramatically.

Because she doesn't spend hours every day hauling water, she has time to garden, which has improved her family's nutrition. She was able to sell some of the extra produce and used the money to buy goats. She's helping to lift her family out of poverty. She also joined a Sunday school class at her church, which was not possible when she was hauling water every Sunday.

Naomi said her relationship with her husband improved because they had become partners in generating income for the family. Sheepishly, she said their intimacy had also improved because of better hygiene. I really loved seeing Naomi laughing, playing with her children, and having leisure time to spend with them.

After capturing her transformed life on video, we asked Naomi to take us to the water source she used to collect from. We drove instead of walking, and even the drive took quite a while. The water source was an open well about eight feet across. The sides were lined with loose rocks, and the water level was about ten feet down. A scum of blue-green algae covered the surface of the water as well as the rocks closest to the water line.

I asked Naomi, "Could you collect water just as you used to, before you got a water point in your village?"

Naomi climbed down the rocks, but when she got near the last row, she stopped. I could see fear in her eyes. I thought maybe she'd seen a snake.

"Come on back up," I urged.

When Naomi rejoined us, she explained, "Many people have slipped on the rocks, particularly after rains, and fallen into the water. Because they don't know how to swim, many times this resulted in drowning." To make sure we got the point, she repeated, "Many people have drowned in this well."

After taking a break, Naomi volunteered to go back down into the open well and collect the water for our video. She went slowly and carefully. We made sure she was never in danger.

After this, I thought we had everything we needed for an excellent video. We would be flying home that day, and the idea of calling it a wrap felt good.

Often when you see videos of this type, you hear the voice of a narrator telling the story. This was originally what we had planned for Naomi's video. But something told me Naomi needed to narrate the video herself. People needed to hear *her* voice—no one else's.

This posed a problem because we didn't have a script, and Naomi didn't speak much English. So if she was going to tell her own story, it needed to be written, translated, approved, and recorded, and we were almost ready to leave.

When we stopped for lunch under a mango tree, I took a pen and my little notebook and walked away from the group. It was hot, flies were all over me, and time was running out. So I prayed, earnestly—a desperate prayer for inspiration. I prayed God would show me how to make this work.

And he did.

Everything Naomi had shown me in our two days together—I wrote it all down in a few minutes. But the words that came didn't sound like *my* words. They seemed like they were *her* words, the way she had told us her story.

Here's what I'd written in my notebook:

> My name is Naomi Nalokae. I am a Maasai woman, a mother of three, a wife, and a sister. I am proud to be a Maasai woman.
>
> My life used to be very different. I used to wake up early and walk all day to fetch water. I had to climb over large rocks to reach the water in the well. I was always so afraid that I would fall in and drown. Many, many people have drowned in that well.
>
> I would waste seven hours every day fetching that dirty water—water that wasn't even safe to drink and made us sick.
>
> I was never clean because there wasn't enough water to bathe. This made my relationship with my husband difficult.
>
> When World Vision brought clean water, things began to change. The new water kiosk is very close to my house. What used to take seven hours now takes seven minutes. Everyone in my village now has clean water.
>
> I love my time with my children and my friends. My dreams for my children have changed now that we have water nearby. They'll go to school and get a good education.
>
> I thank God for my life as a Maasai woman.
>
> I thank God for changing my life by bringing clean water.
>
> Everyone in Kenya and everyone in the world deserves clean water. Women everywhere understand the need for clean water.

This seemed like it reflected well what Naomi told us and would say, and we reviewed the script with her to make sure she agreed. She did, and we recorded her voice for the video. We packed up and headed to the airport. I didn't know if I'd ever see Naomi again, but I was profoundly grateful to have met her.

When we combined Naomi's voice with the video images taken at the well and with Naomi spending time with her friends and family, we had a powerful resource to help people see the transformation that was possible when clean water was accessible. We launched the video in time for Mother's Day, and thousands of people learned Naomi's story.

During my first meeting with Lani at the Boulder hotel, she agreed to go to Kenya to meet Naomi. Kathryn Compton and I traveled with her.

I was eager for Naomi and Lani to get to know each other. Also, Naomi hadn't seen the video we had made about her, and I wanted to show it to her. The best place to do this was in her home, where we could have some privacy. But when we arrived, the moment just didn't feel right. So I suggested we visit the water kiosk World Vision had provided in this community.

The kiosk was a hub of activity. Women and girls were gathering water, and men and boys were herding cattle and goats to drink from the water basins. Soon we gathered in a large circle outside, next to a few cows, and started a conversation with members of the water committee. This committee was made up entirely of tall, imposing men.

The president of the water committee in Naomi's village shared how clean water made their cattle produce more milk and how they collected a water usage fee from everyone in the community. He added proudly, "We created a pipeline to share water from our borehole to three other kiosks in nearby communities. And we have plans for a fourth."

I introduced Lani. "She owns one thousand kiosks in the United States."

Lani shared, "We also charge a water usage fee and set aside enough money to maintain the equipment. We monitor each kiosk remotely with computers so we'll know if there are any problems."

The men's eyes were wide. I suspect this was the first time in their lives they had heard from a woman who was so successful and knowledgeable about water systems.

As the conversation continued and the men became more comfortable with the new dynamic of conversing about business with a woman, the topic turned to how water had affected the village for women and children. At this point, Naomi stepped into the circle and spoke up.

"Clean water enables girls to get an education," she said. "They don't fall behind because of having to haul water every day."

It was a privilege to witness Naomi's strength in speaking up in this male-dominated circle.

Then I knew the time was right to meet with Naomi privately and show her the video. She led us into her home, a mud hut. It was dark inside, cramped, surprisingly cool, and smelled like smoke due to a small open firepit in the middle of the hut. Lani is five foot two, and she had to duck to get through the opening of the doorway. At six foot two, I barely squeezed through. The entire hut couldn't have been more than twelve feet long by six feet wide.

Lani, Naomi, and I sat side by side on the bed, which was a platform slightly raised above the dirt floor. There was something small on the bed, and it was so dark that I was nervous I was going to sit on a child. But to my relief, the only "kid" sharing the bed was a baby goat.

As our eyes adjusted to the dark, the three of us shared about our lives in simple sentences. In her own space, Naomi seemed more empowered to try her English. We were able to understand each other.

Naomi talked about some of the changes that had taken place in her life. She said, "God is an important part of my life, and I love to go to church. But it wasn't possible to attend very often when I had to spend so much of my day fetching water. I am so happy to be able to worship and attend church with clean water close to our home."

I asked, "Would you like to see the video we made of you last year?"

Sitting between the two of us, Naomi held my smartphone (possibly the first one she'd ever used) tightly with both hands. The world seemed to stop. All I could hear was her breathing and the occasional shuffle of the baby goat. Then I pressed Play.

Naomi heard her own voice and saw images of herself, her children, and her friends and neighbors. She saw her struggles before the clean water came and how her life had been transformed, all unfolding right before her eyes on a tiny screen. *Her* story, narrated by her own voice.

As she watched, she kept saying two words over and over. "It's true. It's true."

After the video finished, we were all still. In the stillness we prayed together. I felt the presence of God in that hut in a profound way I've only experienced a few times.

All three of us wept. The huge differences between our lives in the United States and Kenya melted away. We were simply three human beings of equal value, loving our God.

Lani's "kicking the tires" with World Vision convinced her to continue to invest in our water work. Over the next few years, she traveled to see our efforts in several countries, and I was able to join for several of these trips.

Then came the season when, after nearly thirty years, Lani decided to sell her company. She told me she wanted to make a substantial donation to World Vision out of the proceeds. One day, while she was driving, God spoke to her and told her the amount he wanted her to donate. The number was so big—much bigger than what she had been thinking about giving—that she had to stop the car.

Since my days with P&G, and even more so since beginning with World Vision, I had been learning from some of the world's very poor about how present God is with us when we are in need. Beginning with Lani and continuing with other major donors I was privileged to get to know, I learned new lessons from some of the world's very wealthy about listening to God in order to be part of his work in meeting the great needs of our time.

Lani grew up on a farm, and not surprisingly, she's frugal and has learned to squeeze every penny she can. I've seen her spend five minutes getting the last drops out of a bottle of hand lotion. Given the size of the investment God asked Lani to make, she felt an enormous responsibility to make her donation count, and it took a while for her to discern what this might look like.

Lani had a passion for empowering women and girls and saw firsthand that providing clean water was foundational to enabling them to have choices they didn't have when they were hauling water all day. When she learned about World Vision's effective efforts in economic empowerment, she began to think about how she could synergistically invest in women and girls, water, and economic empowerment. She found her answer through World Vision's Strong Women Strong World.

Strong Women Strong World is World Vision's movement of women, men, and young people using their voices and resources to drive change and improve the lives of women and girls globally.[4] It also equips and empowers philanthropists to be a voice for women and girls in the developing world through funding efforts to provide clean water and through enabling better opportunities. The goal is to help end extreme poverty by ensuring half the people in the world are not held back.

After much discussion, Lani agreed to help design and fund a multimillion-dollar investment over three years in a special effort called Beyond Access. This effort included behavior-change strategies to help men and women reimagine their relationship with shared responsibilities based on women's time and effort being freed up by providing clean water. With this emancipation from the work of hauling water, World Vision's economic empowerment could be more successful. This work includes training women in business skills, organizing them in savings groups to pool their money to start and expand their businesses, and providing microloans through World Vision's VisionFund.

In launching Beyond Access at World Vision's Global Women's Summit, Lani said,

> My hope is that in the future, we never have to do this again. Because one day, we will all be equal, and women will be measured by God, not by man. We'll be heard without shouting. Girls will sit in the front of the classroom every day without exception because their generation is not fetching water. As a woman entrepreneur, I know we will multiply because resourcefulness is what we do best. My hope is built upon the love of Christ where the invisible become beautiful.[5]

16

EVERYONE, EVERYWHERE

At a moment when Chris Glynn and I happened to be alone, sometime near the end of 2017, he said he had something to tell me in confidence. "Rich is retiring next year."

The news wasn't a total surprise to me, since our president Rich Stearns had been with World Vision since 1998 and was nearing seventy. I would miss him and so would many others. He was not only an admired leader and beloved friend to those of us who worked for him, but he was also well known nationally, in part for his award-winning book *The Hole in Our Gospel.* News of his resignation, when it was released, would gain a good deal of publicity.

Now, for a nonprofit like ours, a transition of this sort is not just a chance to say goodbye. It's also an opportunity to remind people of our critical work and seek additional donations to complete that work. Chris and I—and certainly Rich—knew this fact well.

"What would you think about doing something extra special tied to Rich's retirement announcement?" Chris said to me.

"What do you have in mind?"

Chris recalled a speech Rich had given the year before at one of our conferences, where Rich had talked about the importance of our big aspirational goal to reach everyone, everywhere we work with clean water. I had been there and remembered the speech well. Rich had joked, "Even if you have to wheel me out in a wheelchair, I want to be there when the last water point is provided by World Vision."

Chris went on. "What if we picked one country and set a goal to reach everyone, everywhere World Vision works in that country with clean water? Then we could ask donors to help fund this plan to honor Rich."

I knew instantly this was not just a good idea but a *huge* idea. Why? Because it's disruptive.

Years before, while I was still at Procter & Gamble, I had learned about disruption from Lee Clow, an advertising genius who was responsible for some of Apple's most iconic advertising. Lee helped us understand that to do something disruptive you have to understand what an industry is doing and then do exactly the opposite.

Ever since then I'd had a fondness for disruptive ideas, maybe because of a contrarian streak in my personality. Professionally, my own most disruptive idea up to this point had been the choice to pursue a nonprofit clean drinking water program within the for-profit P&G.

In the case of providing clean drinking water through an organization like World Vision, the standard approach is to ask donors to fund the work, then later show them the impact, and after that ask them to fund more work. By our communications, we reinforce the idea that the work is never finished because we ask for more money, for essentially the same purpose, year after year. I knew we had a Lee Clow–worthy idea if we could instead ask donors for a fixed amount of money, do the work, show people we had *finished the job*, and tell them we would not ask for any more money for that particular goal.

For a guy who had joined World Vision to expand his impact on the global water crisis that affected hundreds of millions of people, the idea of having an achievable strategy for reaching everyone, everywhere gave me chills.

World Vision would be applying this idea, at first, only in one country, and in that country only in the areas where we had a presence. Yet the concept could be reapplied over and over again, both by World Vision in places where we worked and by others elsewhere. It was like I could see down the corridor of time to this idea, or variations of it, being spread and repeated until everyone in the world had clean water.

"I'm all over it," I told Chris.

I developed all the messaging around Chris Glynn's idea, including using the phrase "Finish the Job" to describe what we were trying to achieve. From the beginning, while I viewed announcing Finish the Job at Rich's retirement as smart from a business perspective, I was more focused on how the bigger strategy of finishing the job would continue long after the retirement announcement. But first we had to start somewhere.

We looked at several options for the first country where we would finish the job, and we picked Rwanda. Located in East Africa, Rwanda is called the land of a thousand hills and is a lush, green country. There's lots of water available in springs, streams, and rivers. The challenge is to get the water from those sources to where people are living. To collect water, many people walk down steep paths from the hills where they live and farm to the valley floors below. By collecting water in large tanks in the valley floor, World Vision can treat the water and then pump it through pipelines up to collection points near people's homes.

To reach everyone in all thirty-nine sectors where we were working in Rwanda meant a lot of water points and a massive amount of piping. But there were several good reasons for choosing Rwanda as our first Finish the Job country. Even when I had come to Rwanda to prepare for Bill and Chelsea Clinton's visit at the very beginning of my World Vision tenure, I had seen that our operation in this country had a strong relationship with the government. That kind of cooperation with civic leadership would be necessary to get approvals (and hopefully some funding) for our work. Also, World Vision Rwanda had an excellent team leader in Sean Kerrigan. Sean understood and valued water work, having moved over to Rwanda from the water team.

We estimated the plan would require World Vision to reach one million people with clean water and require us to raise thirty million dollars from US donors. Up to this point, Rwanda had been a middle-of-the-pack country in terms of water work and fundraising. The numbers we came up with for Finish the Job Rwanda were vastly beyond what we had achieved in this country before. They sounded like God-sized numbers. They would take more than mere hard work to reach. They would require God's intervention, and I liked that.

We developed the Finish the Job plan with a very small team because we needed to keep Rich's retirement plans confidential until they were announced. We were not able to do all the vetting and collaboration we would normally do for a major effort, particularly with the broader technical team. This would soon cause more problems than I would ever have imagined.

But in blissful ignorance of what was to come, I helped launch the Finish the Job Rwanda effort on World Water Day, March 22, 2018. In the written offer to donors, I said, "By getting the job done in Rwanda, we will change the way people think about philanthropy and Africa." Most people didn't believe it was possible to make huge advances in development, particularly among people in deep poverty in Africa. Finishing the job would create a new paradigm for development work.

While in my mind this initiative should have been a cause for celebration and uniting our teams around a common goal, I quickly realized this was not the case. I shouldn't have been surprised. I remembered the words that Dr. Louis Sullivan had said to me many years earlier. "Greg, you will know you are doing disruptive work when you are under attack."

We held our water forum in April 2018 at a hotel in Kigali, the capital of Rwanda. About one hundred people were in attendance, including our leadership, World Vision water staff from around the world, and a dozen donors to our water work. We convened this forum every year to review results, share best practices, disseminate innovations and partnerships, and plan for the years ahead. Of course, this time the new goals for Rwanda were a major topic for discussion.

Before coming to Rwanda, I'd asked to review the technical team's presentations in advance to ensure our messaging to donors was clear and consistent. I'd not received any response and was a little worried about this, but I figured I could provide my input on the day before the presentations.

Once I was in Rwanda, I said to a junior member of the technical team, "I need to review the presentations before the start of the meeting tomorrow. Please send them to me."

She looked at me like a deer caught in the headlights, not knowing how to respond and so not saying anything.

I said, "Is there a problem with that?"

She continued just staring back at me.

I tried again. "I need to see the presentations—we have critical donors in attendance, and I'm responsible for messaging to them."

Finally, she responded softly, "I've been told to not share them with you."

I had sudden flashbacks to when I'd been left out of meetings at P&G to discuss the future of the fledgling water purifier program. Those memories still rankled, and that contributed to my feeling furious at what the junior team member had said to me. Still, I knew she was just following instructions. It would do no good to argue with her.

I tried to get the presentations from her superiors but had to resort to sending emails since they were in partner meetings. My emails were ignored. Before I knew it, our donors had arrived, and I needed to focus on time with them.

Unfortunately, as I had feared, many of the presentations were confusing to our donors.

We had received the results of an evaluation by the University of North Carolina–Chapel Hill indicating a need to improve our sanitation and hygiene work. The report revealed that World Vision's performance in this area was just as good as that of other NGOs, but this fact wasn't communicated well in the presentation. Based on the report, our technical team concluded that we needed to make sanitation and hygiene a higher priority, even if it meant sacrificing the impact we had planned in providing new water points.

I strongly disagreed. Sanitation and hygiene were important, but again, we were performing at a level that matched other NGOs, and I believed nothing should derail the work we were doing with Finish the Job to bring clean water to people who didn't have access.

After the presentations, I asked for a meeting with our technical team leader to try to resolve our differences.

"Why did you refuse to let me see the presentations?" I asked.

He responded, "We have concerns that you view everything through a marketing lens and, if you would have changed the presentations, our technical team would not have understood our need for improvement."

He continued, "You come from the private sector and don't really understand development. You try to push our teams to do too much, and my role is to prevent that."

His comments caught me off guard. I'd always felt that my unique talents were a combination of both marketing *and* scientific skills. *Am I pushing too hard?* I wondered. I didn't think so, but I had always been so driven by my purpose that I sometimes missed how the people around me were affected. His comments caused me some self-doubt. I left Rwanda frustrated.

I shared my concerns about not having a voice in the presentations with my superiors, but nothing much changed afterward. Finish the Job Rwanda required buy-in from many people if it was going to succeed, and some of the people it depended upon had different priorities. I was concerned because I believed they weren't doing what we needed to do if we were going to meet our goals. For weeks turning into months, my frustration mounted. I was at a loss for what to do.

Everything came to a head in July of that year.

At World Vision, major donors are not just people who listen to appeals and write checks. They're true strategy partners involved in how we establish our objectives and go after our goals. It makes sense—to a large extent, it is their money in play. Besides, we value their expertise and their sensitivity to God's leading. I don't know of any other organization where donor involvement in outcomes is present to such an extent as it is at World Vision.

In the water division, we had semiannual reviews with our largest donors, Dave and Dana Dornsife. They were the foundational givers to World Vision's water work, enabling us to create five-year business plans to accomplish our goals. They'd provided $35 million for our first business plan from 2010 to 2015. Then they'd provided another $40 million to take us from 2015 to 2020. Their funding was critical to our commitment to reach twenty million people with clean water by 2020 as well as our plans to finish the job in Rwanda.

Although I was on vacation in Grand Cayman with my family when the semiannual review came up in July 2018, these reviews with the Dornsifes were mission critical, so I left my family at the hotel pool and joined the Zoom meeting from our room.

Once again, the technical team did not share their presentation with me prior to our meeting. The technical team leader shared with the Dornsifes, "We are at 26 percent of target for water beneficiaries." In other words, halfway through the year, we had accomplished only a quarter of the work we had designated for that year.

I cringed when I heard this.

The data presented, while true, was misleading. It is not at all unusual for semiannual achievements to be lower than 50 percent due to annual planning, contracting, and large procurement orders taking place in the first part of the year. In addition, rainy seasons occur mostly in the first half of the year in many African countries, slowing our progress at providing water points. More work *always* gets done in the second half of the year. So when the team leader said we were at 26 percent of where we needed to be, it wasn't good news, but it also wasn't far from the usual midyear benchmark.

We had not shared these details with Dave Dornsife in advance. He responded after the presentation, "We're not meeting our targets, and this is concerning."

The technical leader made an excuse. "We need to increase our impact in sanitation and hygiene, and this new focus may mean we have a lower impact in reaching people with clean water."

The technical team was still stuck on the idea of reorienting our priorities away from Finish the Job, which was confusing to our major donor.

All in all, we made a terrible showing.

Dave ended the call with a crystal clear message: "The Dornsifes will not continue to invest in lower impact."

I felt stunned. I paced in my hotel room, going over the meeting in my mind and wondering if I'd really heard what I thought I'd heard. After providing tens of millions of dollars, were the Dornsifes threatening to stop their funding? The flow of new water could occur only if a flow of money happened first, and while gifts of all sizes were important to our work, the Dornsifes' investment was critical to our being able to do what we had promised.

Within a few minutes, I received a call on my phone. It was Sam Jackson, our lead fundraiser. He said, "Greg, I just had a brief follow-up call with the Dornsifes. Dave and Dana are serious about potentially ending their funding. They've never suggested this in our twenty-five years of working together."

The situation was just as bad as I'd thought.

Sam and I talked a short while, and then I went back to pacing.

It was hard to underestimate what might now go wrong.

If the Dornsifes cut their funding, the vision of "finishing the job"—first in Rwanda and then hopefully elsewhere—could be forgotten. In fact, to a large extent, the water work everywhere World Vision had a footprint was at risk. Instead of reaching more people with clean water than we'd ever imagined, we were now in danger of reaching *fewer* people than in previous years. If worse came to worst, it was possible that water could again become a lower-priority piece of World Vision's development work, just as it had been before I joined the organization.

I opened the curtains and looked out at my family enjoying the tropical afternoon by the pool. Not more than an hour earlier, I'd been enjoying it with them. Now all I felt was desolation.

The ripple effect on the world's poor if the Dornsifes did what they suggested was the most important thing to me. Helping developing nations have access to clean water was the purpose that had animated my career for well over a decade. But, I have to admit, I couldn't ignore the repercussions it might have for me, personally.

A significant reason World Vision had been able to create a

position for me in the first place was because of the Dornsifes' funding. If their funding stopped, then my position would probably be cut as well. And since I had been ineffective in influencing the water team to course-correct, maybe the organization would be right in parting ways with me. In recent years I'd established a strong record of accomplishments, but it felt as if I were back to the kind of failure that marked my early career.

The possible loss of a paycheck didn't matter so much. What about the mission I believed God had called me to all those years ago? What about everything that had happened since? Was this journey really about to come to an ignominious end *now*?

I groaned and laid my forehead against the glass.

Once I was feeling up to it, I went back to the hotel pool to rejoin my family. I sank into the lounge chair next to my wife.

Elaine asked pleasantly, "How did the call go?"

"It was a complete disaster," I told her. "The presentation made it look like we've been dramatically underperforming our goals. And because the Dornsifes now think we're not meeting our goals, they've threatened to stop their funding. All the momentum we've achieved might go away. As I said, it's a disaster."

"Wow, that *is* a disaster," Elaine said. "I'm sorry, Greg." She thought for a minute. "But don't you think World Vision will see how serious this is?"

I thought about that. People weren't listening before, but I bet they would listen to a major donor's concerns.

Despite the disaster, I realized there was still hope for change. There was still hope that we would finish the job.

17

FINISHING THE JOB

The possible loss of funding for World Vision's water work was devastating. I knew that things needed to change at World Vision if we were going to finish the job. But I also realized that things needed to change in *me* first.

Introspection and reflection are difficult when I'm in constant motion. I'm an achiever, and I like to get things done. When I finish one task, I immediately move on to the next one. The disastrous meeting with the Dornsifes put the brakes on my efforts to keep moving, keep achieving, and I began to examine my whole journey so far in helping bring clean water to the world. Things I'd only dimly understood, and in fragmentary fashion, began to form a more coherent pattern in my mind.

As I looked back over my life, I realized that I was ideally situated to be involved in the work I was doing. From my early fascination with Jacques Cousteau and Jane Goodall, I had a love of science—but not the kind of science done in a laboratory. I was interested in scientific tools that could be applied to solve real-world problems. I craved adventure that would take me to new places, and I cared about helping people. Not only that, though—I also cared about messaging. It was hard to get people excited about science-based solutions if they couldn't understand them. All my years at Procter & Gamble, including my appearance on *Oprah* and my marketing work on P&G brands, helped me to understand the importance of getting people to buy into solving the global water crisis. And of course, none of that would have been possible if, as my scoutmaster long ago told me, God hadn't saved me for some purpose. When I thought about my life in sequence, I saw that, even before I had discovered my purpose all those years ago by a contaminated watering hole in Kenya, God had been preparing me for this work.

And then, when I looked back at the critical moments on my career journey, I realized God had been directing the whole thing. While my identity had changed in some ways to "Dr. Allgood, Water Expert," I still was just a water boy, doing God's bidding, even though I had believed it was my skills that led to the things I'd accomplished.

As I was reflecting on God's leading, I realized I'd misinterpreted God's words to me in Geneva—*Do you doubt I can do this?* At the time, I thought "this" was God enabling me to create the not-for-profit effort within P&G. But the truth was that he could do his work with or without me.

There were so many moments in my career that I took credit for but were, on reflection, acts of God—miracles he had allowed me to witness.

How was I arrogant enough to believe that my smarts were responsible for keeping the P&G manufacturing plant running, when millions of packets were already stockpiled and starting to expire? That decision allowed us to have a massive response ready for the southeast Asia tsunami. While I made the decision to keep the plant running, I believe God answered my prayers to guide my decision, and the result was a miracle that helped hundreds of thousands of tsunami survivors.

Then I thought of the *Wall Street Journal* story that changed attitudes about the P&G nonprofit packet program within the company. It wouldn't have happened if God hadn't woken me from a nap in a taxi, despite my extreme exhaustion, to remind me to return a journalist's call.

I remembered how each and every element of the God-sized "five years from the future" vision I'd written for Don Tassone had come true, including being praised by presidents and kings. For me, writing that vision had been a corporate exercise. I hadn't believed it would really come true.

Even the boardroom encounter with A. G. Lafley and Charlotte Otto had God's hand on it. Whenever I told that story, I made it seem that I had panicked and thrown the picture of Mercy into A. G.'s lap. But that's not the way I react to adversity. I don't panic; I focus. I now believed God had made that picture fly out of my hand and into A. G.'s lap—the picture that narrowed the focus from a global problem to a family's need.

I'd already learned that prayers brought me to World Vision from P&G, so why hadn't I figured out that God was directing the organization's water work? And if God had led *me* so powerfully to this work, hadn't he done the same for every person on our teams? I wasn't the only one with a purpose to bring clean water to the world's neediest people. God was orchestrating the whole thing. *He* was the President of Water.

And then there was the series of miracles leading to Lani's big gift, such as me taking a sip long enough to let David Clark tell me about Lani, and the sense of God's presence in Naomi's hut that changed Lani's life and mine. In all this, it was clear that I was God's instrument—no more or less than God's water boy.

This was a revelation to me.

All my life I had been trying to prove myself, to work harder than anyone else to avoid failure. I was excessively ambitious, and I'd always been quick to fend for myself. I would try to take control into my own hands. If I could control it, I could make it work all on my own. But my high school teacher Ms. Thomas had been right—I *did* need more than my own smarts to succeed.

So now . . . I let go. Now that I saw how God had been leading me all along, whether I was aware of it or not, I found that I could willingly receive God's leadership. I could submit to him, trust him, *follow* him.

My pride in my own accomplishments was replaced with profound gratitude and a sense of fulfillment in serving a higher purpose. This was hardly an original or unique perspective, yet it was like I was getting to it for the first time. God could accomplish what I could not. The responsibility for solving the global water crisis was not on my shoulders. Rather, I was just one person God was using to fulfill *his* purpose. How freeing! How peaceful it felt!

My reaction to problems had always been to get to work at solving them. Obstacles were to be overcome, and I was the one to do the overcoming. But now, when Finish the Job Rwanda and the rest of World Vision's water work were on the line because of an ultimatum from major donors, I knew that what would save us wasn't my actions alone.

Our leadership responded to the challenge of the Dornsifes' warning. Our new president and CEO, Edgar Sandoval Sr., called for an all-hands-on-deck response, and we treated it like an organizational crisis. I was formally given responsibility for revised messaging and review of presentations for future forums. It took until October 2018, but everyone was finally on the same page with regard to the technical community's concerns for our plans in Rwanda. The technical team voiced that Finish the Job was a huge stretch for the team, and the rest of us acknowledged their concerns while pledging to support them in the work.

The Rwanda plan would have come crashing down were it not for our leadership standing behind the idea. God was teaching me about how my role was to fulfill *his* purpose and not the other way around. It seemed to me that the Dornsifes and World Vision's leaders, as well as our technical team, were fulfilling God's purpose in bringing clean water to millions, and it wasn't about me at all. Dr. Allgood and his superhero cape were not indispensable.

With this new understanding, I was eager to see what God would do in Rwanda and beyond with the vision he'd given us to finish the job.

The Dornsifes, for their part, felt heard in their concerns. They acknowledged the changes we made and agreed to continue funding our water work.[1] For our next six-month report, we delivered strongly on the goals we had set. And now we were a go on our plan to reach one million people in Rwanda with clean water and to raise thirty million dollars from US donors. We gave ourselves five years.

In the first year, Rwanda country director Sean Kerrigan needed to build up the water team within his country to accomplish this audacious goal. We then planned to double the number of people reached in year two, double again in year three, and keep at that pace the final two years to reach everyone. This would mean Rwanda would need to become one of the top-performing countries out of our entire forty-one-country portfolio—a big task for a small country.

Sean brought over Marie Nicaise Ugabinema from his health team to lead the water work. Marie Nicaise is a capable technical leader, but unsurprisingly, she felt overwhelmed by this far-stretching goal. She set about doing the best she could to help the people of Rwanda access clean water, and her best was very good.

The fundraising goal was perhaps even more stretching than the technical one. Prior to our announcement of Finish the Job, we funded water efforts in Rwanda based on when people gave us funds to use where they were most needed, in whichever country we thought the dollars would have the biggest impact. But in this case, we felt so strongly about the appeal of this disruptive idea that we decided to not use any of the where-most-needed dollars for Rwanda. We needed to go from a baseline of zero to thirty million dollars.

Donors responded positively to our plans. By the end of the second year, we were a little ahead of schedule, having cash in the door or commitments for fourteen of the thirty million dollars needed. Then fundraising slowed down significantly, and I worried we wouldn't meet our goals. I helped host a group of donors on a visit to Rwanda to hopefully regain some momentum.

We had quite a few donors from the United States for our May 2019 trip, including Gerry and Jennifer Rogers, Steve Brannon, Jim Funk, and Matt Manzari. There was also a small team of our US staff.

We started each morning with a different person leading a devotional. In our first devotional, staff member Doug Taylor challenged us to notice how God showed up during our trip. At the end of each day, we'd all take turns sharing how God had showed up for us.

On our first day visiting the areas where World Vision was working, we met Esther and her family. Esther was eight years old and took us to her water source. We walked to a low-lying area where water had gathered in a small pond. She showed our group how she collected the water in her jerrican. The water was dirty, and because we had walked past many cows and dodged a lot of cow poop on the way, we knew the water was contaminated. A familiar scenario, with familiar results.

Esther said, "I miss school almost every month because I get sick from the water. I pray for God to give my village clean water."

Gerry commented later how he could tell that Esther and her friends had low energy and seemed to be without hope for their future. That was understandable, given her sickness and having to do the long walk for water every day.

I took Gerry and Jennifer aside. "We have a plan to bring Esther's community water within the year," I told them. "Would you tell the community the good news?"

They agreed to make the announcement.

The people in the community had already gathered, probably assuming we were ready to say goodbye to them. Gerry thanked the community for allowing us to visit. When it came time to tell the community they'd soon receive clean water, Gerry became emotional. "With God's help," he told them, "World Vision has a plan to bring you clean water by the end of the year."

Immediately the community erupted with cheers.

Gerry noticed an elderly man sitting silently on a porch. He approached the man and asked, "What are you thinking?"

The man said, "You have no idea of the positive impact you will have on our community."

Gerry told me this was one of the most gratifying things he'd ever experienced—on a similar level to the birth of his children and his marriage to Jennifer.

We all felt God had showed up in that holy moment when the community heard they were getting clean water. After Gerry and Jennifer saw up close what clean water meant to the community, they were all in on making sure we finished the job. As Gerry said, "We need to experience the final hallelujah."

The next day, we visited a school and a health-care center that World Vision had reached with clean water. We met with a water committee to hear how they were ensuring the sustainability of their water point. We sat on wooden benches and plastic chairs near the backside of a building. We didn't know it then, but it was the backside of a church. The chairperson of the water committee gave an animated presentation of their efforts.

As our group asked their final questions, Matt Manzari asked our local staff host, Jimmy Gahima, if he could address the small crowd.

Matt is one of the most amazing people I've ever met.[2] He's a retired professional wakeskater and twice nearly died. In one of those near-death experiences, he was electrocuted while trimming trees at a church project, and fourteen thousand volts caused severe burns all over his upper body. His injuries required seventy-eight surgeries. Yet now, by the grace of God, he was back on his feet.

Jimmy gave Matt the go-ahead. We had no idea what he was going to say. Matt told me later he felt called by the Holy Spirit to speak. He told the crowd about his accident and showed them some of the burn scars on his body.

"Everyone has scars," Matt said. "God can help us heal those scars."

I noticed that four of the young men on the hillside were transfixed by Matt's words. This was apparent to me both because of the intensity of their gaze and because it was unusual to see young men so engaged.

Matt asked Jimmy if he could ask if anyone wanted to give their lives to Jesus. Jimmy was initially reluctant—at World Vision, we tell people we're serving them because we follow Jesus' example to serve the poor. We partner with churches whenever possible, but we do not do altar calls ourselves. We leave that to local believers. Matt doesn't do altar calls either, but he felt a prompting of the Holy Spirit to do so here.

After Jimmy's initial reluctance, he felt a nudge to allow Matt to ask.

Matt asked the crowd, "Does anyone want to give their life to Jesus?"

When Matt issued his invitation, four people came down—the same four young men I had noticed earlier. Matt asked our group if anyone knew what these new believers should pray. Doug hesitated but then stepped forward and asked them to proclaim their faith in

Jesus as their Lord and Savior and to ask for forgiveness of their sins, which they did.

We were grateful to be on the backside of the church because some of the church members were close by to shepherd these new Christians. We were also grateful God had allowed us to be part of such a special moment when we sensed the Holy Spirit was moving.

On the last day of our trip, the tour group gathered for lunch and to say goodbye to the Rwanda team. As Doug had encouraged us on our first morning, we each shared where we had seen God show up.

During our conversation, Steve Brannon told the group, "I'm selling my business, and I hoped God would help me see what is next in my life. He hasn't yet." Steve had fallen ill near the start of our visit and had spent most of the trip recovering, so he had missed several of the moments that were highlights for the rest of the group.

Based on what the other donors had seen, they expressed their commitment to help World Vision finish the job.

When our lunch was finished, we bowed our heads and held hands for a final prayer time together. When I thought we were finished praying, I looked up, but I saw that Steve was still praying, and his face was flushed. He was weeping.

As the others opened their eyes, we all looked at Steve expectantly.

When Steve was finished praying, he said, "God just spoke to me."

"What did he say?" We were all eager for Steve to tell us what he had heard.

"He told me," Steve said, slowly and quietly, "that I'm supposed to give a multimillion-dollar gift to finish the job here in Rwanda."

Now it was *our* turn to be stunned. But our shock quickly turned to excitement. We talked for a while about what that funding would mean for people like Esther.

"Did you have any idea you were going to do this?" I asked Steve.

"I'm as surprised as you are," he answered.

Others had given generously as well, but Steve's gift made him the largest investor in our effort to finish the job.

We were all in tears of joy. Marie Nicaise, who is normally calm and almost academic in her demeanor, was sobbing. We hugged.

She told me, "I would not have believed donors from the United States could care as much as I do about providing Rwandans with clean water."

Water points coming to remote areas. People giving their lives to Christ. God prompting generosity to fund our Finish the Job campaign. I was stunned to watch miracles happening right in front of me, God coordinating matters through his people—together.

With the May 2019 trip, Finish the Job regained momentum.

But in early 2020, the COVID-19 pandemic hit.

Rwanda is the most densely populated country in Africa and has limited health care, and many of its people have a low immune status because of widespread malnutrition. So the Rwandan government knew COVID-19 could take a devastating toll. They responded with a complete shutdown, including World Vision's work setting up new water points.

Because of the focus on handwashing to prevent the spread of the virus, and because of the expertise of World Vision engineers, the Rwandan government provided an exemption for World Vision to do some limited work providing permanent handwashing stations in all of the Rwandan hospitals that didn't have them. This exemption later spread to providing handwashing stations in schools and churches, which were not allowed to reopen until they had such stations. We took great satisfaction in helping people gather to worship through this work.

When restrictions eased a bit, the Rwandan government, in recognition of the critical importance of clean water for health, gave World Vision an emergency exemption to restart our water access efforts. We also received additional funds from the Rwandan government to ensure schools and rural health-care facilities had handwashing stations, and we reached more than two hundred of both during this period.

The COVID-19 pandemic stopped our in-person donor meetings. We quickly pivoted to meeting with donors by Zoom. We offered them "virtual trips," with our local staff helping us "visit" beneficiaries over video.

With our pivot to virtual engagement with our donors, Patricia Heaton—the Emmy Award–winning actress from *Everybody Loves Raymond* and *The Middle*—agreed to cohost an event with me where we shared the story of a woman in Rwanda we had been able to help. (Patricia is a World Vision Celebrity Ambassador and serves on the council of World Vision's Strong Women Strong World.) We also shared the success of the first district where we'd finished the work by having Jimmy Gahima on the ground celebrating in a community, with our donors joining virtually. These efforts allowed us to close the gap on our fundraising efforts despite not being able to meet with donors face-to-face.

Going into the Christmas break of 2020, Bill Bryce, one of our senior fundraising staff, asked me to meet via Zoom with one of the donor couples he worked with. He said I should be ready with the latest numbers from Rwanda. This couple asked for an update on the work, and I told them how it was going.

They were encouraged by what they heard and asked, "How much funding do you still need?"

"$1.85 million," I said.

"We've got you covered."

And just like that, we had completed the thirty-million-dollar fundraising effort to finish the job of providing clean water in Rwanda.

I told them tearfully, "You are an incredible Christmas blessing to the people of Rwanda."

It was nothing short of a miracle that we had successfully raised the funds needed for Rwanda in just three years, ahead of the five years we had thought it would take—*and* in the midst of a global pandemic. I was grateful to God for all those who had given gifts—large or small—to complete this huge undertaking.

I took great pleasure in writing that month's newsletter for our donors, informing them we had finished the funding. I added, "To our U.S. donors: Please do not send any money to World Vision for our plan to reach everyone, everywhere we work with basic clean water access in thirty-nine sectors of Rwanda. . . . It is not often that a nonprofit asks you not to send money, but we're all about working ourselves out of a job."[3]

The branding people who reviewed my newsletter strongly objected to my wording. The approach of telling people not to send money seemed too risky to them.

I elevated the decision to Chris Glynn and Edgar Sandoval Sr. Like me, Edgar is a former P&Ger. He and his team at P&G were responsible for the Always brand's "Like a Girl" campaign that helped change people's mindsets about girls' abilities. Edgar understood the disruptive nature of our efforts and the appeal of finishing the job. He not only approved the newsletter, but he also recorded a video that went out with it. "Thank you so much for your generosity, especially in this most unusual year," he told donors.

We had finished the funding, and thanks to heroic efforts by

Marie Nicaise and her team in Rwanda, we were catching up on our work in the field. We were successful in doubling our impact in year two and then doubling again in year three, putting us on schedule to finish the effort. The Rwandan government, having been thoroughly briefed on our plans at the beginning and having given their official approval from the very top, funded 40 percent of the work and signed off as we completed each sector.

Once we passed the threshold of reaching one million people, we held an event attended by Edgar Sandoval Sr. as well as local stakeholders and government leaders.[4] One spring day in 2023, on a big green field, thousands of people turned out to celebrate, hear speeches, and see local dancers. Edgar led a group of schoolchildren in a chant of "One million! One million! One million!" in celebration of the one million people we had successfully reached with clean water in Rwanda.[5]

Our World Vision team met with Rwandan Prime Minister Édouard Ngirente to let him know we fulfilled the commitment we had made to him and the Rwandan people five years prior. He told us, "We congratulate World Vision on setting a big goal five years ago to reach one million people and then exceeding the goal. Many groups set goals but not many beat their targets."[6]

As I spoke to our workers on the ground, I learned that to finish the job, we had provided 3,286 water points and 1,648 miles of piping. These figures were stunning to me. When I was in Rwanda, the land of a thousand hills, it was easy to see the challenge of moving water from the valleys up to the places where people lived, but I had no idea of the massive mileage of piping our team had constructed. This amount of piping would stretch from Boston to Key West! I was grateful to our technical team for rallying around this effort.

The goal to finish the job in Rwanda was a God-sized task. We were successful because God spoke to our donors, and he showed us what all of us on the World Vision team could do. I'm so glad we didn't give up on this new idea of reaching everyone, everywhere in a nation where we worked. And I'm so glad *I* didn't give up or insist on trying to do it all myself. If I had, I would have missed this miraculous work of God.

18

A GOSPEL WITHOUT HOLES

I'd like to be able to say truthfully that I joined World Vision because it is a Christian organization, but that was just a bonus to me at the time. I wanted to join forces with World Vision because of its success in providing clean water. Only over time did I come to fully appreciate their Christian motivation and to be personally impacted by seeing the gospel in action day after day.

World Vision serves every person we can, of any faith or none. We respect the dignity of all people, so we do not exploit the vulnerability of the people we serve or use our programs to coerce conversions. At the same time, our core motivation is to follow the example of Jesus in serving the poor and to demonstrate our faith boldly and humbly.

Through our Christian identity and presence, we witness in ways appropriate to each context, with the hope that people will see Jesus in us and be drawn to him. We serve alongside the poor as a demonstration of God's unconditional love for all people and in response to Jesus' call in Matthew 25:40 to serve "the least of these my brothers and sisters." Not surprisingly for a water boy, one of my favorite Bible verses is Jesus' words in Matthew 25:35: "I was thirsty, and you gave me a drink."

I believe the faith shared by World Vision staff makes us more effective in our development work. Most of the world's people are religious, and that's particularly true in areas where World Vision works. As a Christian organization, World Vision is well positioned to work with local religious leaders of all faiths as agents of change and advocates for the importance of clean water, improved sanitation, and healthy hygiene behaviors.[1]

When you combine World Vision's faith basis with its focus on helping children reach their full, God-given potential, then you can literally transform communities. I've witnessed this in hundreds of communities where World Vision works, and it's the reason I feel blessed to work for World Vision and to also be a donor.

While we were finishing the job in Rwanda, we were preparing to do the same in Honduras and Zambia. In Honduras, we were encouraged to create the plan by our donors, including Cody Nath and his company RTI, Barry and Linda Rowan, and Joe and Amy Wu. It was in Zambia that I received some of the strongest reminders I've ever encountered of both the need we were addressing and God's ways of meeting that need.

Kenita and Allen live at the end of their road in a rural community in Zambia. The group I was with in the summer of 2023 had an appointment to meet with them there. COVID-19 restrictions had mostly gone away by this time. I was traveling with many of the same donors I'd visited Rwanda with prior to the pandemic, including

Steve Brannon, Gerry and Jennifer Rogers, and Jim Funk (who was now joined by his wife, Sherree). We were also joined by Doug and Geni Garrison.

Kenita and her family were living in extreme poverty. Their clothes were tattered, and they didn't have shoes. We heard how old the children were, and we saw they were very small for their ages, their growth stunted from poor nutrition. When Kenita introduced her five children, she told us they had lost one child to severe diarrhea. Her children were listless, and one of them was currently recovering from diarrhea. Kenita said one or more of her children had diarrhea almost all the time.

Kenita explained she collected water four times every day from a water hole about a mile away. We offered to help her collect water and set off as a group.

When we got there, I was appalled. The water hole was an open well about five feet across. I looked down into the well and saw the water level six feet down. By now, I had seen thousands of contaminated water points, but this was one of the worst. The water had the color and consistency of milk. It smelled awful. There were cattle everywhere, and the community had put sticks over the open well to keep the cows from falling in. I heard they were not always successful and occasionally had to pull a cow from the well.

As we collected water, four women from the community arrived with their water containers. I greeted them and asked, "What do you think about this water? Is it contaminated?"

They looked at me like I was not very bright.

"What do *you* think?" one of the women asked. "*Look* at this." She pointed at the cow poop surrounding the well.

"It's hard to even drink this water, because of the smell," another woman told me.

I decided now would be a good time to share some news we had been holding back. I asked Doug and Geni to tell the good news.

"This community will soon have a new water point," Doug said.

Kenita and the four women looked stunned and remained silent for several seconds. Then they broke into a song and started splashing water from their buckets onto themselves. Our local World Vision Zambia host, Mutinta, translated their words. They were singing an impromptu song about how this would be one of the last times they had to wash in the nasty water.

Our team struggled with the weight of the water on the way back to the village.

Jennifer asked Kenita, "How do you manage to carry the heavy water?"

She responded matter-of-factly, "These are just problems."

Kenita was living in extreme poverty and clearly cared deeply about her family. She took her suffering in stride. Kenita understood, probably better than her visitors, that our lives on earth are short and full of suffering. The way we respond to challenges makes all the difference. Our group was inspired by Kenita's resilience.

When we returned to her home, our tour group was visibly exhausted. Kenita immediately said, "Are you ready for a second trip?"

We froze. *Another trip?*

Kenita smiled. "I'm just joking."

We all laughed. But Kenita's joke was a reminder of the hard work she had to do four times every day.

She asked us to sit so she and her husband could thank us for the good news of the coming water point. "I wish I could open my heart for you to see how it's overflowing with the blessing you've provided to us," Kenita said. "Tell me about the water points in your country."

The request caught me off guard, and I wasn't sure how to respond. "In the States, we have water piped into our homes," I sheepishly told her.

After a pause, Gerry chimed in. "In fact, water is available in many rooms of our house."

Kenita seemed amazed at this. Four grueling trips to a filthy well and back per day, and we could get clean water on demand virtually anywhere in our house.

We continued our conversation, but the injustice of the situation sat with us. We were reminded that everyone deserves clean water and that solving the global water crisis is something that not only can but *must* be done.

The entire group was moved by our experience at Kenita's home and in her village. At a hotel restaurant the next day, as we were debriefing what happened, Jim Funk proposed that the donors on the trip split the cost to fund the water point in Kenita's village. Once they had seen firsthand the conditions she was facing, they felt motivated to act.

"Elaine and I want to be part of this effort too," I said.

Then something miraculous happened, something no one in the group had planned. It was like the Holy Spirit was speaking to each of us around the table in turn. Everyone had the sense that we were part of a work God was doing in Zambia.

Doug and Geni Garrison had been moved by the group's experiences over the last several days, particularly telling Kenita and her family they would receive clean water. And even though they had told us prior to the trip that, for their own personal financial reasons, they would need to take a break from giving at high levels, now they said they would make a substantial new donation to the Zambia effort.

Gerry and Jennifer Rogers and Steve Brannon considered the Garrisons' commitment. They had both been impressed by our work in health-care centers and agreed to fund several more.

Jim and Sherree Funk put their heads together, used the calculator on their phone, and then told the group of a new and impactful donation they would make.

Steve finished this amazing night by saying he felt led by God to make another big commitment. After conferring with his wife, Sandy, Steve made the same level of sacrificial commitment for Zambia that he had previously made to help finish the job in Rwanda.

I wish I could convey in words what all this felt like. I was deeply moved by this generosity, and yet it was more than that. As each of these new and unexpected gifts was being made, I could feel the presence of God in a powerful way. It was a confirmation that God sees and cares for the poor, and he was moving in our hearts to be the answer to their prayers. I felt blessed to be a part of what God was doing.

I asked our World Vision Zambia staff to arrange for the group to experience a water celebration while we were there. The pink of a beautiful African sunset was just starting to appear on the horizon as we walked up a hill where the community had gathered around the drilling rig. The community greeted us with singing and dancing, and we joined in the celebration.

I enjoyed the dancing, but it seemed to be going on longer than normal. *Shouldn't we see the water by now?* Then I noticed I was not hearing the usual noises from the drilling rig. I went to Mutinta and asked her what was up.

"Doc, the compressor isn't working," she told me.

The dancing stopped. We all stood around, hoping the team could get the problem fixed.

After about fifteen minutes, Mutinta came to me and said, "It's still not working. Doc, you need to lead us in prayer for the compressor."

My mind started racing. I was surprised she suggested that *I* do it. People don't usually ask me to pray, maybe because I'm not the most approachable guy. I thought, *What if I pray and it still doesn't work?* That would be a disappointment for the community as well as for the donors. It seemed like praying would make me vulnerable if God didn't answer. Should I agree?

But while I was thinking, I was surprised to hear myself say, "Let's do it."

While our drilling team continued working on the compressor, I gathered our team into a circle and prayed. "God," I said, "if it's your will, please start the compressor and bring clean water to this community today."

I finished the prayer.

Nothing happened.

Three of our World Vision staff—the area program manager, one of his staff, and one of our drivers—had been standing behind us during the prayer. Now they started singing "Be Still and Know That I Am God."

Be still and know that I am God . . .

The rest of us fell silent while the men sang. I was nervous that my prayer hadn't worked and was looking around to gauge how others were feeling. I knew what clean water meant to the community, and I didn't want to let them down. I knew I needed to trust God, but also I wanted him to show up in a mighty way for these people.

I am the Lord that healeth thee . . .

By the second verse, the people had bowed their heads, and a few others had joined in the singing. I bowed my head too. I thought of Kenita's statement that one or more of her children were almost constantly sick because of dirty water. I knew the Lord cared for these people, and I silently prayed that God *would* heal them by bringing the clean water they so desperately needed.

Then the men began the final verse.

In Thee, O Lord, I put my trust . . .

For so much of my career, I had expected God to work on *my* terms. I was working toward a worthy goal, so I thought God should bless my every effort. But I realized then, standing in the waning daylight of the Zambian sun, that I am not capable of performing the work on my own. I couldn't fix that compressor, and I wasn't on the ground in Zambia, living in the community, preparing them for the clean water that would one day arrive. God works on his timetable and on his terms, not mine. Based on what I'd witnessed on this trip, I made that final verse of the song a prayer over my life and my work. *In Thee, O Lord, I put my trust.*

As the men sang that final verse, we heard the compressor cough and sputter, then crank up to full speed. The people erupted in cheers.

A few minutes later, the water was gushing high overhead with the beautiful glow of the sunset behind it.

I stood in awe of the miracle God had allowed me to be part of.

Then Gerry and I joined the community under the spray in this celebration of life transformed. It felt almost like another baptism to me, washing away my sins and proclaiming my faith.

I was glad the community saw us praying for God to bring clean water. I was glad they saw that the water came when the local World Vision staff were asking for God's intervention. I'm certain this story will be told for generations in this village and remembered as a turning point when they began to prosper.

I later learned of a postscript to this story, which Robin Folkerts, the Funks' World Vision donor representative, shared with me.

During our trip, she was in the United States and was reading a book with a bookmark that displayed the words from Psalm 46:10: "Be still, and know that I am God." Every day, Robin saw the bookmark and prayed that phrase over our trip. Afterward, Robin heard how our staff had sung "Be Still and Know That I Am God" before the compressor started working. We were amazed the Lord was providing the same message in two different places at the same time. Robin called this a "God wink," as if God was letting us know it was his plan all along.

I've had a lot of amazing trips in my time at Procter & Gamble and World Vision, but this trip to Zambia will always be set apart as the "miracle trip." Combined with the way God overcame the obstacles to Finish the Job, seeing him act powerfully in Zambia and other places among both the very poor and the very wealthy solidified my trust in him.

19

NO TURNING BACK

I've been blessed to have many friends in my lifetime, but two have remained closer to me than any others. As teenagers, Wes Williams, Don Glenn, and I would run through each other's houses like they were our own. We'd get together for pickup basketball games and all kinds of hijinks and hanging out. As grown men, we'd keep in touch about our careers and families. Every time I'd fly back to North Carolina to see my family, I'd see Don and Wes while I was there. And after I resolved on Mount Kilimanjaro to spend more time on the relationships that were important to me, Don, Wes, and I would set aside time each year to take trips together.

Sometimes we would go hiking in the Rocky Mountains, based out of my home in Boulder. Or we'd go kayaking in North Carolina, often staying at Wes's condo on Sunset Beach.

On one of our kayaking trips, I had been thinking I needed a plan for when I die.

Around the time of the second Summit on the Summit, I was in South Sudan with one of our clean-water partners, PSI. As we walked through a refugee camp near the Nile River, a boy came up and pointed a toy rifle at me only a couple of feet from my head.

"It's not nice to point guns at people," I told him and pushed the barrel of the gun away. The boy walked off.

A few minutes later, when we jumped in our vehicle, I noticed my host looked shaken.

"What's wrong?" I asked him.

"That gun you pushed away? That wasn't a toy. That boy could have killed you."

I'm not sure whether my naivete had put us in danger or saved us, but I was thankful God was watching over us.

Because of this and other experiences, and because my adventurous lifestyle had led to several accidents and injuries already, I figured there was a good chance that when I die, it will be unexpected. By the time of the kayak trip, I wanted a plan in place. So when we took a break from paddling, I suggested that Wes, Don, and I make a pact. "Guys, whoever passes first, the other two have to say a eulogy at the funeral."

This was my selfish plan to be covered in the event of my sudden death.

"Yeah, yeah, okay," the guys agreed.

Later the same day, I navigated us up and down narrow coastal creeks behind Bird Island, near Sunset Beach. We got really lost. Finally, not long before sunset, and with miles to go before getting home, we found a wide channel we believed would take us back to our launch. But after following it for more than a mile, it narrowed, narrowed, and then ended.

Wes was exhausted, and when he caught up to me, he cried out, "We've gone too far to turn around now!" We laughed, knowing we had no choice but to go back the way we'd come. Yet this phrase became our friendship mantra. When it came to our commitment to each other, we really had gone too far together to turn around.

Recently, perhaps because at this season in my life I receive frequent reminders of how finite life is, I've done a lot of thinking about my past and what my life amounts to, about the transitory nature of existence and the importance of what we do with our limited time on earth. My actions have been far from perfect, but my eyes have been opened to the abundant evidence that God has been working in me anyway. Today, my life and my mission as a water boy are not yet done. But that time will come, and I'm not afraid of it.

While I've spent many years in parts of the world where suffering and death are (unfortunately) all too common, the deaths of two people near to me have brought the idea of finishing well into sharp focus.

In September 2021, as my colleagues and I at World Vision neared completion of the Finish the Job Honduras planning, I went to visit Wes and Don in North Carolina.

I'm accident prone and had fractured my foot, so I showed up for the trip wearing a boot. That temporary injury paled in importance, however, beside another fact: Wes had recently been diagnosed with ALS (also known as Lou Gehrig's disease). This news was heartbreaking to all three of us, but particularly to Don, whose mother had died of this disease after an eleven-year battle. Don and I had decided that a trip to Wes's condo on Sunset Beach would lift Wes's spirits. Wes was already starting to tire easily, so Don and I spent some of the time with Wes and then, while he was resting, some of the time kayaking, just the two of us.

On the first day, the three of us walked the short distance to the beach. Don, far ahead, chuckled at his two pals who took forever to hobble over. Wes was now in braces for his legs, and pain in my foot slowed me down.

When we made it to the shore, I took off my boot, eased into the water, and swam out beyond the nearby pier. Suddenly I was struck by the tentacles of a Portuguese man-of-war. Similar to a jellyfish but more venomous, a man-of-war packs a powerful wallop. I screamed in pain and immediately headed back to shore. Wes and Don could see the welts across my chest from the venom of the tentacles. They could also see that although I was in pain, I was okay. As friends often do, they laughed at my misfortune, which cheered me up. "Great form swimming back," Don said.

The next day, Don and I headed out for a day of kayaking. I left my boot in his truck and hobbled to my kayak. We had a marvelous day of chasing the tides deep into the coastal creeks behind Bird Island, all the while keeping Wes updated with texts and pictures.

When it came time for a break, Don and I landed our kayaks on a sandbar. I stretched out my arms and legs and relaxed by floating in the water. Then I was stung *again* by a Portuguese man-of-war. Twice in two days—what are the chances? This time was worse, and the tentacle welts covered both my arms and chest.

When it was time to head home, we returned to the place where we'd left our kayaks and paddled back. The tide was low now, and the launch spot was a shallow, mud-covered bottom. Getting out of my kayak, I slipped and instinctively pulled in my leg with the injured foot. Just imagine the tuck a figure skater does to achieve a spin, and that's what happened. I did a quick 360-degree turn, something I could never pull off if I was trying. My good foot then went out from under me, and I landed hard on my side. I heard a *crack*—my rib.

I had a broken foot, two sets of Portuguese man-of-war stings, and now a broken rib.

Don looked at me, shook his head, and said, "You're a mess."

Thanks, pal, I thought. But he was right. I felt renewed justification for the pact I'd coaxed Don and Wes into.

Don loaded the kayaks back onto his truck while I crawled—muddy, broken, and stung—into the passenger seat.

When we got back to Wes's condo, I went to the guest room and turned on my phone. The first thing I noticed was a WhatsApp message from Javier Mayorga.

Javier was the leader of the World Vision Honduras water efforts, making him a key figure in our Finish the Job Honduras plans. Javier had an infectious personality with a wonderful smile and was a favorite of donors visiting Honduras. I'd been with him recently at World Vision's World Water Forum, where he was thrilled to be among his water colleagues.

Javier wanted me to know the team had completed the planning to finish the job in Honduras. He messaged, "We can do it!" It was great to hear from him because I knew he was in the hospital with COVID-19. The night before, he'd sent a message asking me to pray for him.

Then I looked at my phone messages and saw I had missed a call from Amy Thompson, World Vision national director of philanthropy. She and I had taken many trips to Honduras and had met with Javier. I didn't know why she would be calling me and figured I'd better call her back. "Hi, Amy," I said. "I saw I missed your call. What's up?"

"I'm sorry to have to tell you this, Greg," she said, "but Javier passed a few hours ago."

I tried to take this in, but it was overwhelming. It was hard to imagine someone so vibrant and full of life as Javier dying.

When I hung up, I couldn't keep my composure any longer. I wept for my friend.

Wes was coming down the hall slowly in his braces and heard me sobbing. My dear friend came into the room and sat with me as I cried for Javier.

After I had traveled home, Wes told me our visit *had* lifted his spirits. Even with the devastating news of his ALS, it helped him to be able to grieve with me.

World Vision employees and donors mourned Javier's passing and committed to finish the job in Honduras in his honor. Javier's last words to us became our rallying cry: "We can do it!"

But Wes's diagnosis, my own injuries, and Javier's unexpected death were bringing home to me the fragility of life.

The following summer, Don flew out to join me in Boulder for one of our annual hiking trips in the Rocky Mountains. Wes's ALS was steadily progressing, and he couldn't join us this time. It was just Don and me, although Don brought along a life-size headshot of Wes to show in photos that he was there with us in spirit (a practice Don and I continued for each of the trips Wes couldn't make).

After a warm-up day of hiking around Boulder, we headed out for 14,036-foot Mount Sherman. I'd had three stress fractures in my foot in a row, starting with the one that had put me in a boot for the previous year's kayaking trip. I thought I'd recovered from the last of these fractures. Unfortunately, the day before Don arrived, my foot started hurting again. The morning of our hike, I had extreme pain in my foot. Don suggested we abandon the hiking plan, but I insisted we continue.

Although I have a high pain threshold, this shooting pain with every step was almost more than I could take. I suppressed many screams, but when we ascended through a mile of loose stones, I cried out with every step. Making our way along a narrow ridge near the top, I *crawled* through the most dangerous part. With relief, we took some pictures at the summit, had lunch, and started down.

The pain of descending was even worse than going up because of the greater pressure on my toes from the gravity of my downhill weight. Exhausted and spent, we reached the car.

Our plan was to spend the night at a hotel in Buena Vista and then hike Mount Massive, the second-highest peak in Colorado. While we were walking in Buena Vista that afternoon, I suddenly felt faint. I made it to a bench where you can watch river surfers on the Arkansas River. I said to Don, "I'm going out." I crumpled and fell to the ground.

Don was alarmed and noticed I was not breathing. He couldn't find a pulse.

Just as I had done with Brandy in Fiji, Don called for me to return to him. "Greg, come back. Come back to me." Over and over.

I eventually regained consciousness.

"Are you okay?" Don asked, worried.

I couldn't speak. I wasn't sure what was wrong with me, so I wouldn't have known how to respond even if I could have.

Finally, I managed to say, "Water."

While Don ran back to the car for water, I started to hallucinate. I saw a young couple finish surfing the Arkansas River, get out of the water right in front of me, and have a conversation about getting together later. Then I saw it again. By the third time, I knew exactly what they were going to say and then heard them say it. I thought I'd lost my mind and was in some kind of recurring loop.

Don brought some water and a bottle of Gatorade from the car. I had looked at my watch when he left, and I looked again when he returned—I thought it was now earlier than when he'd left, and this added to my confusion. I felt certain time was moving backward.

I was still on the ground but managed to hold the water bottle Don offered me. I took a few sips and realized I was extremely thirsty.

I motioned for Don to hand me the Gatorade and drank the entire bottle.

The river where I fainted is right behind the Surf Hotel, and Don ran to the hotel for help. The hotel concierge called 911. An EMT team responded quickly and hooked me up to an IV. They took me in an ambulance to Salida Hospital. I was in and out of consciousness during the transport and subsequent draws of blood. One test came back with an out-of-range value for troponin, indicating a possible heart attack. This local hospital didn't feel equipped to handle the situation and transported me by helicopter to a hospital in Colorado Springs, over a hundred miles away.

I continued to hallucinate during the helicopter ride. I imagined we were flying up to a big net across the sky and had to descend quickly to find a way around it.

The Colorado Springs hospital repeated the lab work and took blood samples every hour through the night. All the testing showed normal values. The cardiologist didn't think I'd had a heart attack, so I was released from the hospital.

Don and I spent hours afterward reliving this incident, trying to understand what had happened. Medically, the best explanation is probably severe dehydration associated with physical exhaustion from my climbing the mountain with the injured foot. But it seemed strange to Don and me that I'd had such a strong reaction to this. Of course, the irony of the water boy almost dying partly because of dehydration didn't escape me.

This incident changed us. After this experience and my vulnerability, Don and I were able to share our feelings with each other in ways we never did before. Our previous conversations had focused more on sports, politics, and trips we were planning. But now we also shared our struggles. We encouraged each other, provided advice, and lovingly challenged each other in areas where we thought the other person should consider a different approach. We both said that these conversations led us to take different actions than we would have taken otherwise. I felt blessed to have such a dear friend. Looking back now, I feel God was bringing us closer so we were prepared for what would happen in the not too distant future.

I'd made mistakes throughout my career by not making family and friends a priority, and I'd learned from my errors. During the COVID-19 shutdown of 2020, Don, Wes, and I had started having weekly phone calls to check in and talk. Even after the shutdown, despite a rigorous travel schedule with World Vision, I made time for these weekly calls, and we texted frequently. Wes had told us about his ALS diagnosis during one of those calls.

A few days before Thanksgiving 2023, Wes stopped responding to my texts and calls. I felt God telling me something was wrong. God's voice did not seem like a whisper but was strong, keeping me up all night. In the past I might have suppressed what I was hearing or written it off as my imagination. But after everything I'd seen, this time I listened and acted on it.

In the morning, I called Don, who lived near Wes, and asked him to check on our friend.

Don called later and told me the news. "Wes has taken a sudden turn for the worse. He's lost the ability to speak." He paused. "Greg, his family called in hospice."

When the hospice workers arrived and examined Wes, they told Wes's wife, Jennifer, that it would probably be three to four weeks before Wes passed but that in these situations the timing was uncertain.

Based on the three- to four-week estimate, I could have delayed making a visit to Wes. But based on the prompting I'd already received, I jumped on the next flight from Denver to Raleigh-Durham. By that afternoon, Don and I were holding Wes's hands and sharing memories with him. We told him, as we had many times before, "We love you, Wes. You've had a bigger impact on our lives than you realize."

And it was true. Wes had always been there for Don and me. We called him "Two Shoes" in high school because we knew he was the guy who would always do the right thing. But even though he did the right thing, he never judged Don or me for our mistakes or said, "I told you so." He was the first person to help us get back on our feet. He was dependable, always there for us. So we wanted to be there for him and his family.

I haven't always known what to say or how to act in these situations. At times my restlessness and thirst for adventure have pushed the people around me harder than I intended. But my journey in spending time with suffering people and listening to God enabled me to be there for Wes and his family. Over and over, during those last days, Don and I seemed to have been put in their home at just the right time and led to do exactly what was needed most.

Late Friday afternoon, I sensed Wes's suffering as he was struggling to breathe, even with the CPAP machine assisting. I thought Wes might be undermedicated. Both Don and I had worked in the health-care field and did some quick research into safe dose levels. We learned Wes's medication could be increased significantly and still be within the margin of safety. Hospice was not scheduled to come back until Monday, so we encouraged Jennifer to call them to confirm the change in dose.

We had this conversation in front of Wes and realized he was listening. So I asked him, "Wes, are you okay with this? Do you trust these two knuckleheads?" A slight smile came to Wes's face, and although he couldn't speak, he gave us a thumbs-up. Jennifer called, and hospice encouraged Jennifer to increase the dose significantly to reduce Wes's suffering.

Wes's daughters, Megan and Morgan, and Jennifer were overwhelmed with grief at the suddenness of Wes's decline. I realize now that all the qualities that allowed me to respond in my career in times of disaster—focus, quick decision-making, and tenacity—God used to help Wes's family in the quickly deteriorating circumstances of his ALS. They trusted Don and me to help them through difficult end-of-life decisions they didn't have the energy to make. Our being there allowed them to be fully present for Wes in his final days.

One afternoon, I sat with Wes, holding his hand. It was a holy moment, and even though Wes was unable to communicate, I heard God telling me it was time for Wes to go.

I gathered Jennifer and the girls. "He's ready to pass now. We need to let him go."

Later that afternoon, with guidance from the hospice nurse, Jennifer told him, "I know you're tired, Wes. The girls and I will be okay. You can go now." Wes was always so conscientious, and I knew he needed to hear that his family would be okay without him.

A little later, I prayed with Jennifer, asking God to help Wes pass peacefully.

He passed in his sleep that night.

Don and I were back at Wes's house when the funeral home came to collect him. Not surprisingly, it was difficult for Jennifer, and she was weeping. Because Wes had requested to be cremated, she knew this was the last time she'd see him. After she said her goodbyes to Wes, I led her into their kitchen so she didn't have to see the funeral home prepare Wes for transport. As I held her in my arms, I felt God urging me to get Wes's wedding band for her. I sat her in a chair and told her what I was going to do. She stopped sobbing and looked at me. "Yes," she said. "Yes, please." I stopped the people from the funeral home before they left the house, took the ring off Wes's hand, and gave him one last kiss on the forehead.

Jennifer held the ring tightly as the funeral home vehicle loaded Wes and drove away.

Once again, Don and I were at the right place at the right time.

When I had suggested the pact to Wes and Don, I figured I would be the first of us to go. Instead, as we'd agreed on our long-ago kayaking trip, Don and I gave eulogies at Wes's funeral.

I shared stories of the times Wes, Don, and I had spent together. I closed by saying, "We learned to express our love for each other and to share our life's struggles. That's not always easy for men to do, at least not for me, and friendship with Wes and Don has meant the world to me and made me a better person. Wes always kept a positive attitude. In fact, whenever I'm feeling down or overwhelmed in life, I think of Wes and his strength in coping with ALS. Wes will continue to inspire Don and me for the rest of our lives."

My time with Wes and his family somehow made my faith more tangible. God had faithfully provided comfort when I experienced death and suffering through my work. And now God had helped me at one of the times I needed it most, the death of my closest friend of more than sixty years. My time with Wes had also made my faith—which I usually kept to myself—more apparent to others.

Elaine was the first to say something. After Wes's passing, Elaine, in her typical straight-ahead approach, told me, "You've become more spiritual through this process." She had witnessed my care for Wes and had seen how God was using me to help his family.

I might have been able to write off one comment, but then Don (who is on a different spiritual path from mine) told me, "It's hard to believe all these coincidences. You seem changed and more open in sharing your faith. You've become *way* more spiritual."

I also had my annual review at World Vision around this time, and my boss, Chris Glynn, said to me, "I think your time at World Vision has really changed you. You're comfortable in sharing your faith in a way you didn't do when you joined us."

Elaine, Don, and Chris were right. I *had* changed. I could not deny the miracles I'd seen, or the way God had shown up time and again, from the time I was a Boy Scout, hearing God had saved me for a purpose, to the time I was living out that purpose in bringing clean water to those who needed it.

God just kept showing up.

20

SHOWING UP

Elaine, Don, and Chris Glynn were all right: I *was* more open with my faith than I had been. But I had also become much more aware of the places where God was showing up—and of the places where he had shown up all along. Three events helped me to see this in an especially close way.

First, Procter & Gamble invited me to attend the fifteenth anniversary celebration of the opening of the manufacturing plant in Singapore that produced the P&G packets. It would be held on June 18, 2023.

World Vision's Keith Kall and Claude Zukowski, who was leading the P&G program, asked if I had ideas of people whose stories we could revisit as part of the celebration.

Several individuals came to mind, but I had a clear favorite—*if* we could find her.

Grace.

My history with Grace went back more than a decade.

P&G has an initiative called brandSAVER, a collection of coupons for P&G products that used to be included as an insert in over fifty million Sunday newspapers. In 2011, I worked with the P&G brandSAVER team to include a donation for each coupon redeemed. The thought was that consumers could use their purchase of everyday items to make a difference. Each redeemed coupon donated one day's worth of clean water. Because of the massive redemption of coupons by Americans, millions of liters were provided.

We needed compelling photos and a story to accompany the "One Coupon = One Day of Clean Water" offer. So early in 2011 I traveled with Samantha Sakemiller, brandSAVER manager, to an area near Malindi, on the coast of Kenya, where we had an excellent program providing clean water with the P&G packets through World Vision. We visited several homes to see how they were using the packets and scout for someone to serve as the face of the effort.

I noticed a little girl shyly hiding in the doorway of one of the homes. I knew instantly. "That's her." There was something about her smile that just made you want to laugh.

We introduced ourselves to the little girl's mother, Margaret. She told us Grace was three years old.

We went with Grace and Margaret to see where they collected their water. It was a two-hour walk to a filthy, swampy pond. For Samantha, this water walk was a new experience. I had taken many such walks, ever since meeting Mercy at the beginning of my own clean-water journey. These water walks are a crucial part of understanding the reality of the water crisis that millions around the world face.

Margaret explained, "My family and friends frequently suffered from diarrhea. It was often quite severe." She looked down. "Some children in the community have died. I didn't like it when Grace got sick, but we didn't have another option for water. We were forced to drink the swamp water to survive."

But things had changed since World Vision began providing the

P&G packets. Although this community had not yet received a permanent water point, they used the packets to purify their water. The community trusted that the packets worked because they could see the transformation from dirty to clean water. Grace and the other children were no longer getting sick.

Samantha and I had a rewarding visit with Margaret and Grace, and we ended it singing and dancing with the community. By this point in my work, I'd done this so often that I knew exactly what to expect—this was part of my normal experience. But seeing the joy on Samantha's face while she danced wiped away any jadedness I might have felt.

While Samantha had gained approval for us to have the cover of the brandSAVER, our team was not sure that everyday Americans would make the connection between clean water and P&G products. Yet Grace and her smile turned that issue into a major success as consumers purchased many more P&G products than expected. It was clear they *did* understand the impact of their purchase in providing clean water.

I was grateful Grace's smile had enabled us to provide millions more clean-water packets for children like her. But I figured I'd not meet Grace again.

I was wrong.

When we had the idea to reconnect with Grace to help P&G celebrate fifteen years of the manufacturing plant, I visited her again, this time with Claude Zukowski as well as a photographer and a videographer. In 2023 Grace was fifteen years old. She had gone from barely surviving, when I first met her, to thriving. Her family had been in deep poverty when we first met, but World Vision had provided Margaret with training on raising chickens, and now she had a lucrative poultry business. Grace not only was in high school (something unlikely to have happened if she were still hauling dirty water every day) but was enrolled in an exclusive school for outstanding students.

"Do you remember me?" I asked Grace.

"Yes, very well!" she replied. "I remember you making funny animal sounds to get me to smile in the pictures."

I remembered that too.

The community by now had a permanent water point provided by World Vision and so didn't need to use groundwater treated with the packets. But Grace took us to the old swamp and showed us that she remembered how to use them. She was no longer a shy little girl and didn't need my animal sounds to make her smile.

Our photographer recreated the brandSAVER picture, so we had Grace in the same pose at three and at fifteen years of age. We also recreated a picture taken of Grace and me at that time. In the old photos, I towered above Grace; we now could look almost eye to eye. As I looked directly into Grace's eyes, I could see her strength and resolve. I knew at that moment God has a plan for her every bit as much as he had for me.

We showed the photos at the celebration, and something of the emotion of Grace's situation communicated itself to each person in the audience. The clear transformation of Grace's life that all started with the P&G packets strongly resonated with P&G's purpose to improve lives. Grace's story, multiplied by millions of others like hers, showed the power of P&G's commitment to the effort.

It was a blessing to reunite with my former colleagues and to inspire a new generation of P&Gers on the power of clean water work. P&G had by this point provided more than twenty-three billion liters of clean water in the twenty years since the not-for-profit program was started.

The gathering in Singapore was a nostalgic moment for me, bringing back memories of my work during the first phase of my career and the people I'd been privileged to engage in it with. Another moment that reminded me of how God has shown up came in November of that year, when I was honored to receive the P&G Alumni Association John Pepper Humanitarian Award for my work providing clean water through both P&G and World Vision.

I had kept in touch with John Pepper over the years and admired him as much as ever. I'm honored to call him a friend and to have his support in my work.

John had agreed to introduce me for this award but was unable to travel to the ceremony for health reasons. Marc Pritchard, P&G chief brand-building officer, stepped in and recounted how the two of us had honed the strategy for the P&G Children's Safe Drinking Water Program. Marc said, "I met Greg in 2006. I was inspired by his work. I said, 'Greg, let's work together to see what we can do to figure out how we can make this big.' I met with him for a few Fridays, and then he took it from there."[1]

A. G. Lafley, former P&G CEO, was also there. It was fulfilling to be able to say to A. G., "Thank you for agreeing to create the not-for-profit effort for the P&G packets. You asked me to think of the twenty-year plan for the program—and in a few months, the program will be twenty years old."

A. G. smiled. "We made the right decision."

I was also able to thank former CEOs Bob McDonald and David Taylor, as well as CEO Jon Moeller. P&G's purpose of improving lives is part of the company's DNA, and this is demonstrated by the multiple generations of CEOs who continue to champion P&G's water work.

God had spoken to me in Geneva, asking, *Do you doubt I can do this?* I had no idea then what God had in store—for me or for the people in the world he would use me to reach. It was thrilling to consider the impact of what he had done.

The 2024 meeting of World Vision's National Leadership Council, composed of our biggest donors, was held at a hotel in Carlsbad, California. I was asked to give a presentation, which is something that by this point I'd done countless times and typically felt confident in doing. Yet I woke at five a.m. that day and felt I wasn't ready.

I went to the hotel's fitness center and worked out hard for an hour on the elliptical. During my workout, I tried out various versions of the presentation in my mind, trying to go beyond my normal presentation style to provide a more compelling update on our work. Those listening would be donors who had been radically generous to World Vision in the past. I desperately wanted something big to happen to further our water work. We had done so much, but I believed there was still a lot more we could do.

Back at my room, I showered and spent another hour trying to figure out how I should change my presentation. I hadn't worked this hard on a presentation or been this nervous since I'd hyper-prepared for *Oprah* many years before. I typically rehearse by standing and speaking the presentation out loud until it feels comfortable. This morning, I started and stopped over and over, not feeling comfortable with anything I tried. After struggling for hours, I still felt lost.

I sat down. This was going nowhere. I knew I needed God's help.

Rather than praying a desperate prayer asking God to support what I had in mind, as I would have done in the past, I prayed simply, *God, show me what you want me to do.*

After sitting still for a few minutes, I felt the answer come. *Just do you.*

I felt a strong impression that I simply needed to play the role God had given me and not put the weight of the outcome all on my shoulders. God had shown up again and again in a mighty way in the past. In this instance, God wanted me just to *show up* and see what he would do. He would lead.

I absorbed this message and felt calm. I didn't make any further preparations.

On the stage, with the bright lights shining on me, I could see only the first few rows. I shared World Vision's amazing results in providing clean water and improved health care. At that point, World Vision had reached twenty-nine million people with clean water—equivalent to almost the entire population of the state of Texas. And we'd upgraded more than two thousand rural health clinics, providing improved health care to more than eighteen million people.

Next, I laid out the goals of our new campaign with the audience—to reach an additional thirty million people with clean water by 2030 and to upgrade three thousand more rural health-care facilities, including all the clinics everywhere we work in Niger.

"After completing the Finish the Job Rwanda program," I said, "we are committed to reaching everyone with clean water everywhere we work in both Honduras and Zambia. We've raised all but eight million of the fifty million dollars needed for Zambia."

Just then, from a back corner of the room, I heard a voice say, "We'll do it."

I couldn't see the speaker, but I recognized the voice. It was Ryan Lambert, an entrepreneur and philanthropist I had recently met who was attending his first National Leadership Council. His words meant that he and his wife, Holly, would give the eight million dollars necessary to finish the funding for Zambia.

Wow.

Without hesitating or even thinking, I leaped the several feet off the elevated stage and ran to him. I hugged him and thanked him.

Wiping tears from my face, I made my way back onto the stage. I still had to cover our health-care work for the audience.

Resuming my presentation, I explained how we had reapplied

the Finish the Job concept to our health-care work and had recently funded upgrading all the clinics everywhere we worked in Zambia and Rwanda.

"We have ninety-six clinics still needing funding in Niger in order to upgrade all the clinics everywhere we work in that country," I said.

Then I heard from the back of the room "How much would that be?"

It was Ryan Lambert again.

I swallowed and answered hesitantly, "Twelve million."

There was barely a pause before I heard "We'll do that too."

Again, I leaped from the stage and ran back to Ryan. This time the audience was on their feet clapping. I raised my arm and pointed up to Jesus, and so did Ryan. God was showing up. We both wept.

Ryan told me he hadn't planned to give this gift. But as I had been speaking about the needs in Zambia and Niger, he felt God calling him. He had made his decision only a few seconds before telling me. And even after making the first pledge, he didn't know he'd make the second.

The feeling in the room after Ryan's pledges was palpable and holy. Dozens of our donors came up to tell me they felt they'd just witnessed a miracle. Many people were in tears, feeling like God was moving.

A few hours later, our leadership invited Ryan onto the stage, and with their agreement, he issued a challenge. "I'll match any donation that is committed during the next twenty-four hours."

It was unprecedented for a donor to offer a challenge at this meeting, but because so many people in the room felt they had witnessed a miracle, we wanted to give them a way to directly be part of what God was doing. All of us—World Vision staff and donors alike—recognized the great opportunity this was to multiply our work together.

The next day, a few of us gathered in a conference room with Ryan and used FaceTime to have Holly join us virtually. Ryan opened an envelope and revealed the amount our donors had committed to. The Lamberts would match this amount, on top of what Ryan had already pledged the previous day.

Just as I was calculating what this total would come to, Holly—over FaceTime—said to her husband, "Ryan? Ryan, let's do a double match."

I was stunned.

This last gift brought the total giving to over eighty million dollars, a record that remains the largest sum of private donations in any single day in World Vision's seventy-five-year history.

To say that God showed up would be an understatement. He was moving in people's hearts in a powerful way.

I wasn't the only one who fell to my knees to thank God for this miracle of generosity—but I was the first. Tears streamed down my face as I thought of the children who would have clean water because of these gifts. I thought of Mercy, and Grace, and Jemima, and Naomi, and Kenita, and Allen. I thought of the woman who had asked me, "If water was there all the time, why did it take until now for us to have it?" I thanked God that, because of these gifts generously provided, hundreds of thousands more *wouldn't* have to wait.

God had chosen me to be part of this larger story. He had prepared me for it, but he had also used the experiences of the previous twenty years to draw me closer to himself. And through those experiences he had changed me. He had given me a calling, yes, but he had also shaped and developed that calling as I learned more about the global water crisis and how God was moving others—and not just me—to be part of the solution. I had been tempted time and again to be the "blue-eyed prince" rushing to the rescue. Sadly, I had not always resisted this impulse. While trying to go it alone did help others, it unnecessarily hurt those closest to me. But now God was teaching me a better and more effective way. Through trusting in the ways God was moving others, I could be more effective in the role he had given me while also remaining close to those who mattered most.

This substantial gift felt like the culmination of all he had been teaching me. He'd told me the day before, even before the first twenty million dollars had been pledged, that I needed to simply show up and do my part in this story, trusting him for the results. Perhaps this level of generosity would have happened without me—God knows. All I know is I was grateful God had chosen to include me in what he was doing.

Later that same day, I felt I not only truly understood my life's calling but was ready to proclaim it in public for the first time. I was no longer the "blue-eyed prince" who couldn't resist rushing to the rescue as the solo superhero. I introduced myself to a World Vision audience not as Dr. Greg Allgood but as God's water boy.

Epilogue: The Miracle Continues

In 2000, when I first became involved in combating the global water crisis, four thousand children under the age of five were dying every day from diseases related to unclean water, poor sanitation, and lack of adequate hygiene. Today that number stands at about one thousand children per day.[1] This drop in deaths is largely due to the fact that an incredible two billion people have gained access to clean water since 2000. The number of people now lacking access to a basic clean-water source is about seven hundred million.[2]

These numbers prove the global water crisis is solvable. In fact, I believe that we can reach a point where everyone, everywhere on the globe has access to clean water and that we can achieve this goal within our lifetime. After all, we have less distance to go than we've already gone in a quarter century. We just need to have urgency in addressing this issue.

Unfortunately, the world is not easily aroused from its complacency about the global water crisis, because these deaths are so common and because they occur among people in remote areas of the world. But children and adults dying every day from something as simple as the lack of clean water is *unacceptable*. And it is *unnecessary*.

There are a lot of complex problems in the world, but providing a clean-water source in a rural community is not one of them. This is something we know how to do. We have the technology now. It's proven, it's sustainable, and it's cheap. In fact, it's one of the most cost-effective ways to save and improve lives.

Water is fundamental to development. If we don't get water right, then a community will remain in extreme poverty despite anyone's best efforts. But when we get water right, it changes everything. Kids are healthy because they're not sick from dirty water. Their growth is not stunted because of persistent diarrhea. Children can go to school instead of hauling water. Women can be freed from the back-breaking and time-consuming effort of hauling water every day and instead can be more present for their families and pursue new economic opportunities. Individuals, families, and communities will be transformed.

The words that helped inspire me to start my journey with World Vision ring true now more than ever before: With everyone doing their part, according to their own abilities, we can easily solve the global water crisis.

Of course, not everyone has a primary calling to combat the global water crisis like I do. But we all can do something to help! I believe God has something important for every one of us to do within his master plan of good for humanity. My story proves that, if we humbly listen and follow him, our impact will be so much greater than if we try to do it on our own. God has a strategy for reaching the world, and there is work for all of us to do in finishing the job.

Acknowledgments

I've spent many years of my life traveling on planes and bumpy car rides in the developing world. I've flown more than four million miles on Delta alone and made more than sixty trips to Africa. I don't watch where we're going during the long car rides and instead enjoy getting to know my colleagues and donor partners. Indeed, it was during one of those long car rides that former World Vision fund-raiser Doug Taylor and donor partner Steve Brannon asked me to tell them my story of how I came to lead the water efforts at World Vision. After hearing about my successes and failures, they urged me to write this book. I'd heard that suggestion before, but they really pushed me, including following up with me after the trip. I didn't really like the idea, but God used this suggestion to keep nudging me. I had all kinds of worthwhile excuses—not enough time, no experience, and I was most worried that I'd lapse back into bad habits of spending too much time away from my loved ones.

Then God started slowly turning the screws on me. Finally, it seemed I'd go crazy if I didn't write it. Once I started, I truly felt that I wasn't the one writing this book. I was just the scribe. As much as any time in my life, God was leading this process. Thank you, God. And thank you, Doug and Steve, for being God's instruments.

Two people deserve special thanks for getting this book off the ground. My wife, Dr. Elaine Allgood, and Don Glenn. Elaine has learned to understand, sometimes before I do, when God is speaking to me, and she said I should go for it. Thank you, Elaine. I love you. Don is a journalist and not only encouraged me but helped me develop a game plan for this book. He continued to encourage me as some of the more difficult parts of this memoir unfolded for us together while I was writing.

Jim and Sherree Funk, World Vision donors, were the first ones to read a draft of the book, and their encouragement fueled me to continue the process. Rich Stearns, former World Vision US president, who has written many books, including the bestselling *The Hole in Our Gospel*, encouraged me and had many useful suggestions to start the process. Barry Rowan, a longtime World Vision donor who recently wrote *The Spiritual Art of Business*, took me under his wing with guidance, prayers, reading lists, and patience. He helped me understand that my initial draft needed to focus on one theme. After reading my proposal, Dale Hanson Bourke, who has written several books, including *Strong Girls, Strong World*, agreed to introduce me to the folks at Tyndale, and for that I'm deeply grateful. Thank you, Jim, Sherree, Rich, Barry, and Dale. I don't deserve the time and thought you put into helping me.

Thank you to Eric Stanford and Jonathan Schindler for honing the book and helping me dig deep into my feelings. To the team at Tyndale, including Jan Long Harris and Jon Farrar, thank you for taking a chance on my story.

Thank you to the employees of Procter & Gamble with whom I served for nearly three decades. I continue to believe that P&G is the greatest for-profit company on the planet. Thank you to P&G leadership who directly supported the P&G water program, including Susan Arnold, Carolyn Brehm, the late George Carpenter, John Goodwin, A. G. Lafley, Charlotte Otto, John Pepper, Marc Pritchard,

Paul Polman, Jim Stengel, and Don Tassone. Without you, the P&G water effort would not exist.

A double thank-you to John Pepper, who is a saint among us and has sent me notes of encouragement for decades, as well as set one of the best examples I know of a life well lived. I love you, John.

I'm forever grateful to have served at P&G alongside my friends Peg Fortenberry, Victoria Great, Allison Tummon Kamphuis, Samantha Sakemiller, Melanie Suer, Keith Zook, and Claude Zukowski. Together we provided clean water for millions and had a great time doing it. Thank you.

Thank you to Dr. Jamie Bartram, Sally Cowal, Alie Eleveld, Dr. Rob Quick, and Jemima Odo, who taught me so much in the early days of the P&G program.

Thank you to Kenna for curating Summit on the Summit: Kilimanjaro and including me. Thank you to Jimmy Chin for getting me up the mountain with your expert advice. Thank you to Alexandra Cousteau for sharing about Jacques Cousteau, my inspiration to become a scientist, and to Jane Goodall for the same inspiration.

Thank you to Cindy DiBiasi for being my friend and colleague and for helping transform me from a shy scientist to a PR machine.

Thank you to Roy Spence for giving me a multimillion-dollar tagline.

Thank you to former President Bill Clinton, Secretary Hillary Clinton, and Dr. Chelsea Clinton for shining a spotlight on the global water crisis and the work that P&G and World Vision are doing to address it.

I've learned so much about radical generosity from World Vision donor partners, including Robert and Laura Abernathy, Linda Barto, Bob and Karrie Bloomquist, Steve and Sandy Brannon, Lyné Brown and Pat Williams, Scott and Tracy Brunjes, Craig and April Chapman, Vinh and Leisle Chung, Margo Day, Lani Dolifka, Dave and Dana Dornsife, Daryl and Jackie Drummond, Dr. Mark and Carol Feanny, Nick and Mim Frey, Phil and Pati Frey, Jim and Sherree Funk, Christine Gaddini, Doug and Geni Garrison, Earl and Joyce Godwin, Royden Goodson, David and Anne Grizzle, Jeff and Sandy Grubb, Chris Hardy, Patricia Heaton, David and Carla Hillard, Bob and Sandy Hoover, Betsy King, Drs. Rob and Anne Klamar, Harmon and Lea Kong, Ryan and Holly Lambert, Debbie and Wayne Macomber and the LaCombe family, Matt Manzari, Mike and Ruthann Mason, Jeff and Sarah McParland, Gary and Judi Mittelstaedt, Steve and Audrey Monke, Bill and Jennifer Nath, Cody and Christine Nath, Mark and Tricia Ratley, Taylor and Stacey Rhodes, Gerry and Jennifer Rogers, Barry and Linda Rowan, Thom and Joani Schultz, Jim and Janie Smith, Mark and Jennifer Smith, Rich and Renée Stearns, Chris and Kathy Stump, Tom and Sandi Swinford, Don and Carol Sytsma, Joel and Debby Tan, Ed and Sherri Torres, Kathy Treat, Doug and Pat Treff, John and Lila Trull, Tom and Mary Vande Guchte, Barney and Carolyn Visser and family, Carl and Carol Wall, Jay and Judy Welker, Laura Whitley, Chris and Lorraine Wilson, Eric and Jen Wolford, Dustin Wright, and Joe and Amy Wu. Thank you to these and all World Vision donor partners for allowing us to be the hands and feet of Jesus serving the poor.

Thank you to World Vision leadership, including Edgar Sandoval Sr., Chris Glynn, and Sean Kerrigan for your excellent guidance that has helped make World Vision the best place to work to serve the poor.

Thank you to Perri Leung for being a wonderful teammate and keeping the trains running on time.

I love all of the donor representatives at World Vision and couldn't do my job without them, but a special thank-you to my friends Catherine Brazinski, Kathryn Compton, David Derr, Missy Eck, Robin Folkerts, Tony Frank, Randy Haacke, Sam Jackson, Terry Johnson, Erik Joller, Dave Navarra, Deborah Padberg, Andy Pyne,

Debbie Quesada, Lyndsey Deane Ratchford, Dr. Kathy Saunders, Liz Setser, Doug Taylor, Chris Tews, Amy Thompson, Randy Valentine, Mike Vollette, and Jeff Witten for partnering with me.

Thank you to our current and former World Vision water technical team including Idalina Roia Alfai, Dr. Samuel Diarra, Dr. Fungai Makoni, Godfrey Mawaa, Maybin Ng'ambi, Dr. Emmanuel Opong, Margaret Schuler, Jordan Smoke, and Dr. Ray Norman, as well as all of their amazing teams.

A special thank-you to Keith Kall, who was my main connection to World Vision when I was at P&G and continues to shepherd that relationship as well as several other critical partnerships providing clean water to millions.

To all my fellow World Vision colleagues both in the United States and serving in the toughest places in the world, thank you for making World Vision the best place to invest to change the world. Please know that I treasure working with you and seeing your heart to love and serve the poor. It has transformed me.

Thank you to Jennifer, Megan, and Morgan Williams for letting me be part of that sacred time with Wes. And thank you, Wes. I'll see you soon, but I hope not too soon.

For my family. Thank you to Jim and Meriem Allgood and Jeannie Renegar for being there when the clouds were darkest. I love you. A special thank-you to my wife, Elaine Allgood, and our children and their spouses: Ashton Allgood-Batten and John Batten, Meredith Allgood, George and Logan Charles, Shaun Shanahan and Madeline Charles. Thank you for your encouragement and understanding. I pray this book encourages you in your own journeys of purpose. A special thank-you to Ashton and Meredith for loving me despite my numerous failings as a father. To our grandchildren, Kade Batten, Sophia Charles, William Charles, and Zoey Charles, I can't wait to share these stories with you. I love you all.

Thank you to the thousands of people whom I've met personally during my travels to remote places. You have been willing to open your homes, share your needs and aspirations, and share your suffering. You've broken my heart so it could grow bigger.

Thank you to everyone who is reading my book. My fervent hope is that this book inspires you to let God show how he can use you to do miraculous things. Even better if he leads you to join the effort with your time, talents, and treasures to help end the global water crisis. Let's get this done in our lifetime.

Everything in this book is true to the best of my knowledge, and I've been lucky that most of the events are easy to double-check from blogs, news releases, videos, and newspaper stories.

Your Personal Purpose: A Discussion Guide

In *Thirsty for a Miracle*, Greg Allgood tells the story of discovering his life's purpose to bring clean water to the world's poor. In this guide, using Greg's experiences as a starting point, you will reflect on your own experiences, gifts, strengths, and weaknesses and explore what shape God's purpose for your life might take. This guide can be used on your own or in a group setting.

1. Greg was introduced to the water purifier packets at a time when he was feeling restless: His work didn't generate the success he had expected, and he felt eager for a change. Reflect on a time when you have been restless in your personal or professional life. How did you handle that season of uncertainty? What challenges and opportunities did it present? If you found a way through that season, how? What insights did that season reveal to you?

2. When Greg tried to start the nonprofit effort for the water purifier packets, he faced strong opposition. How did Greg respond to opposition? Is there a time in your life when you faced opposition for something you thought was right? How did you react? What was the outcome? What did you learn from this experience?

____

____

____

____

____

3. When Greg was faced with the decision of whether to tell the factory to stop producing packets (because they had a large surplus) or to keep going, he decided to keep going, in case of "a big global disaster" (page 61), which positioned his company to have an effective response in the aftermath of 2004's tsunami. Why do you think Greg made this decision? What factors do you take into account when you have a big decision to make? What role does prayer play in your decisions? How do you evaluate whether a decision was good or bad?

____

____

____

____

____

4. Greg is clear-eyed about some of the mistakes he made—times when he was too tenacious, or put his work before his family, or acted impulsively without considering how those actions might affect others. Think about some times when you've made mistakes personally and professionally. What led you to make them? How did others respond? What consequences resulted from the mistakes? What wisdom did you gain from them?

5. Greg's mistakes seem related to the strengths that made him effective in his work. Make a list of your own strengths. How do these strengths enable you to be effective in your life and work? In what way might these strengths cause difficulties for you or for others?

6. In 2011, Greg was feeling pulled to transition from his work at Procter & Gamble to join World Vision's water program. It was not an easy decision to leave work that he had stewarded for so long and felt strong ownership of. What factors led him to this decision? Have you faced a time of transition, when you had to decide whether to stay or to go? How did you decide one way or the other? If you stayed, how did deciding to stay change your situation or your outlook? If you left, what led you to make the leap to something new? What advice would you give to someone in a similar situation?

7. As Greg looked back over his life, he could see the hand of God directing him. Even things like his love of science and adventure seemed designed by God to lead him to the purpose he eventually found. Think about your own life's journey. As you consider God's purpose for you, in what ways can you see God's direction, God's leading, or God's favor? What gifts has God given you? Use the spaces below to make a list of some of these things.

8. If you feel like you know your calling, how do you see the things you wrote down in question 7 leading you toward it? If you don't feel a sense of calling in your life, how might God be leading you through what you've experienced and the gifts and talents you've been given?

9. After Greg's experience on Kilimanjaro, he resolved to make his loved ones more of a priority, including his friends. Describe Greg's relationship with his friends Don and Wes. How did these relationships grow throughout Greg's life? How did Greg's presence during Wes's final days change him? What relationships have been meaningful for you? How do you prioritize these relationships? In what ways can you further nurture them?

10. Greg writes in the epilogue, "My story proves that, if we humbly listen and follow [God], our impact will be so much greater than if we try to do it on our own" (page 208). Think of the people around you—in your family, your church, your workplace, the organizations you volunteer with, and the places where you spend your free time. What would it look like for you to partner with them in the purpose you've been given? How can you support them with your gifts and talents? How might God be leading you to work with others to accomplish his purposes?

11. Greg opens the book with an epigraph from Matthew 25:35: "I was thirsty, and you gave me a drink." This passage has been an important impetus for Greg's work in delivering water to the world's poor. Read Jesus' words in Matthew 25:31-46. Jesus commends those "sheep" who served "one of the least of these my brothers and sisters" because, in doing so, they "were doing it to me" (verse 40). Conversely, he rebukes those "goats" who "refused to help the least of these my brothers and sisters" because they were "refusing to help me" (verse 45). What does this story reveal about God's heart for those in need? Think about your own life. How are you helping "the least of these"? What opportunities

are open to you to serve "the least of these"? What service opportunities might God be leading you into now? What steps could you take today to be involved in serving "the least of these"?

12. The subtitle of the book speaks to a dual need: for Greg to discover the purpose for which God made him, and for the world's poor to have access to clean water. The purpose that Greg discovered combined a deep need he felt with a deep need within the world. How does the purpose God has called you to (or might be calling you to) intersect with the world's need? How can your gifts, talents, and experiences be used to help others?

Notes

CHAPTER 2: THE OPRAH WINFREY SHOW

1. Center for Science in the Public Interest, "Food Watchdog Michael Jacobson to Change Roles at CSPI," November 2, 2016, https://www.cspinet.org/news/food-watchdog-michael-jacobson-change-roles-cspi-20161102.
2. Activist Facts, "Center for Science in the Public Interest," accessed September 22, 2025, https://www.activistfacts.com/organizations/13-center-for-science-in-the-public-interest/.
3. Greg Allgood, "Research Behind the FDA Approval of Olestra," *British Nutrition Bulletin* 21, no. 3 (1996): 174–182, https://onlinelibrary.wiley.com/doi/10.1111/j.1467-3010.1996.tb00849.x.

CHAPTER 3: MAGIC IN A PACKET

1. We found precedents in, among other sources, C. K. Prahalad, *The Fortune at the Bottom of the Pyramid: Eradicating Poverty through Profits* (Wharton School Publishing, 2004).
2. The *purpose* of P&G is to provide branded products and services of superior quality and value that improve the lives of the world's consumers, now and for generations to come. The *values* reflect the behaviors of the way P&G does business, such as being honest, operating with integrity, and always trying to do the right thing. The *principles* share the approach P&G uses to conduct work, including showing respect for all individuals, placing value on innovation and mastery, and seeking to be the best.
3. Katharine Q. Seelye, "Metamucil Ad Featuring Old Faithful Causes a Stir," *New York Times*, January 19, 2003, https://www.nytimes.com/2003/01/19/us/metamucil-ad-featuring-old-faithful-causes-a-stir.html.

CHAPTER 4: TESTING THE WATERS

1. Procter & Gamble, "Promising New Technology Proven Effective in Purifying Water for the Developing World," press release, June 30, 2003.
2. Erik Eckholm, "River Blindness: Conquering an Ancient Scourge," *The New York Times Magazine*, January 8, 1989, https://www.nytimes.com/1989/02/05/magazine/l-river-blindness-904189.html.

CHAPTER 5: STOPPED IN MY TRACKS

1. See Jemima on YouTube in a video produced at a later time: "Help Us Share—Kenya and Jemima Odo," https://www.youtube.com/watch?v=KAa6y7fgRpQ.
2. As a result of my visit with Jemima, CNN learned about Jemima and produced a story on her. The CNN crew showed up the same week Jemima's husband and son died, but she pushed through the interviews despite her grief because she felt it was important to get the word out—another display of courage and selflessness. I visited her several times, coming to treasure her friendship. I watched as she fulfilled a dream of opening a series of shops before she passed away in 2016.

CHAPTER 8: PLUNGED INTO PROMINENCE

1. Sarah Ellison and Eric Bellman, "Clean Water, No Profit," *Wall Street Journal*, February 23, 2005, https://www.wsj.com/articles/SB110910057933261072.

CHAPTER 9: TWO CENTS' WORTH

1. Stephanie Strom and Claudia Deutsch, "P.&G. Link in Amex Contest Raises Questions of Fairness," *New York Times*, July 28, 2007, https://www.nytimes.com/2007/07/28/business/28amex.html.

CHAPTER 10: PLAYING THE HERO

1. To learn more on the Children's Safe Drinking Water Program or to donate, see https://csdw.org.

CHAPTER 11: SUMMIT ON THE SUMMIT

1. Hillary Rodham Clinton, "Remarks," March 22, 2010, National Geographic Society, Washington, DC, transcript, https://2009-2017.state.gov/secretary/20092013clinton/rm/2010/03/138737.htm.
2. "Kenna, Lupe Fiasco, and Mike Shinoda, Resurrection (Official Video)," posted March 10, 2010, by Illusive Music, YouTube, https://www.youtube.com/watch?v=iwoUF6IMGDE.

CHAPTER 12: GOODBYE, HELLO

1. "Program Provides One Billionth Liter of Clean Water," WaterWorld, April 29, 2008, https://www.waterworld.com/drinking-water/article/16214267/program-provides-one-billionth-liter-of-clean-water.
2. Bill Clinton, Clinton Global Initiative 2011 Annual Meeting, Sheraton Times Square, New York, September 20, 2011.
3. Greg Allgood, "Retiring from P&G and Joining World Vision Water: Continuing the Work to Provide Clean Water to the Poor," *Latest News, Updates from Around the World*, June 19, 2013, https://assets.ctfassets.net/ej38p024hv5h/2IvnisOgdI01d5J5NvdR6o/50b71f1c4de00ea28dcce3c782beb8df/jun-19-2013-retiring-from-pg-and-joining-world-vision-water-continuing-the-work-to-provide-clean-water-to-the-poor.pdf.

CHAPTER 14: TURNING UP THE FLOW

1. The information Emmanuel shared with me in our conversation can also be found in Jeff Walters, Emmanuel Opong, and Greg Allgood, *World Vision's Approach to*

Community Engagement for Sustainable Water, Sanitation, and Hygiene Projects (World Vision International, October 27, 2014), https://www.wvi.org/sites/default/files/WVI_CommunityEngagement.pdf.
2. "Keeping the Water Flowing: UNC Study Commends World Vision's Approach as a Key Factor to Sustainability," World Vision Water, https://www.worldvisionphilanthropy.org/hubfs/resources/Water%20-%20UNC%20Study%202-page%20Overview.pdf.
3. Philanthropedia, "Ranked Nonprofits: International Water, Sanitation, & Hygiene 2011," International Water, Sanitation, & Hygiene 2011 Top Nonprofit Ranking, accessed June 3, 2014, https://www.myphilanthropedia.org/top-nonprofits/international/water-sanitationhygiene/2011.
4. *Survey of the Cumulative Impact of Water, Sanitation, and Hygiene: Implementers' Efforts to Address Global Water and Sanitation Crises* (World Vision Water, March 2015), https://fiscalresearchcenter.issuelab.org/resources/21188/21188.pdf.
5. United Nations, Department of Economic and Social Affairs, "The 17 Goals," https://sdgs.un.org/goals.
6. Kerry A. Dolan, "Big Bet Philanthropy: How More Givers Are Spending Big and Taking Risks to Solve Society's Problems," *Forbes*, December 8, 2016, https://www.forbes.com/sites/kerryadolan/2016/11/30/big-bet-philanthropy-solving-social-problems/?sh=1eb2722079c5.
7. World Vision US, "Water—World Vision Water Point Sustainability," Vimeo, https://vimeo.com/showcase/2832974/video/98938109.

CHAPTER 15: STRONG WOMEN

1. See World Vision Philanthropy, https://www.worldvisionphilanthropy.org.
2. "Clean Water: Empowering Women in Kenya," posted May 5, 2015, by World Vision, YouTube, https://www.youtube.com/watch?v=7hZluhyA2wo.
3. Rick Johnston, WHO, personal communication, July 3, 2024.
4. World Vision, "Women and Girls," https://www.worldvisionphilanthropy.org/women.
5. Lani Dolifka, World Vision's Global Women's Summit, Virtual Zoom Meeting, September 30, 2021.

CHAPTER 17: FINISHING THE JOB

1. At the time of writing this book in 2025, the Dornsife family's total financial commitment to World Vision's water work is an incredible $150 million, including a financial commitment that helped launch our fourth five-year business plan, covering 2026–2030.
2. See Beyond the Burn, https://www.beyondtheburn.life.
3. World Vision Water and Health Newsletter, December 2020, https://www.worldvisionphilanthropy.org/world-vision-water-update-december-2021.
4. See Edgar A Sandoval Sr., "On #WorldWaterDay, I'm remembering a moment that illustrated the power of clean water access," LinkedIn, March 22, 2023, https://www.linkedin.com/feed/update/urn:li:activity:7177193688052178944.
5. By the time all was said and done, we had actually reached more than 1.2 million people.
6. World Vision Water and Health Newsletter, June 2023, https://www.worldvisionphilanthropy.org/world-vision-water-and-health-update-june-2024.

CHAPTER 18: A GOSPEL WITHOUT HOLES

1. As part of our witness through word, we developed a tool to build the capacity of local Christian churches through the lens of water. *Jesus: The Source of Living Water* is a book initially created by Dr. Emmanuel Opong, following a vision he received from God.

CHAPTER 20: SHOWING UP

1. Marc Pritchard, P&G Alumni Global Conference, November 3, 2023, Washington, DC.

EPILOGUE: THE MIRACLE CONTINUES

1. "Water-Related Crises Threaten the Lives of 190 Million Children," UNICEF, March 20, 2023, https://www.unicef.ch/en/current/news/2023-03-20/triple-threat-water-related-crises-threatens-lives-190-million-children.
2. "Progress on Household Drinking Water, Sanitation and Hygiene 2000–2022: Special Focus on Gender," UNICEF, July 5, 2023, https://data.unicef.org/resources/jmp-report-2023/.

About the Author

DR. GREG ALLGOOD is vice president of water and health at World Vision, the largest Christian relief and development organization in the world. Under Greg's leadership, World Vision has reached more than thirty-five million people with clean water since 2016—more than the population of Texas. At World Vision, he championed the effort to "finish the job" and reach everyone, everywhere World Vision works with clean water.

Prior to joining World Vision, Greg worked for Procter & Gamble (P&G) for twenty-seven years and was the founder of the P&G Children's Safe Drinking Water program, the P&G Nutrition Science Institute, and the P&G Health Sciences Institute. He earned a PhD in toxicology from North Carolina State University and both a master of science degree in public health and a bachelor of science degree in biology from the University of North Carolina—Chapel Hill.

Greg has worked with a wide range of C-suite executives as well as celebrities who have supported his efforts. He has partnered with individuals, corporations, and foundations resulting in more than $1.6 billion invested in providing clean water in the developing world. He has created cause-marketing programs used by global brands and retailers to successfully build businesses.

The programs Greg led at P&G and World Vision have resulted in two dozen awards recognizing Greg's expertise in both public health and marketing, including the *Condé Nast* Visionary, *The Economist* Social Innovation Award, Distinguished Alumni of the Year by the University of North Carolina, and one of the top 100 marketers in the world by *Internationalist Magazine*.

Greg lives in Boulder, Colorado, with his wife, Elaine. They have four grown children and four grandchildren.